Acknowledgments

First of all I would like to thank God. Thank You for Your sacrifice and for turning my life around. Thank You for bringing me out of darkness into Your marvelous light. Thank You for giving me the Holy Spirit. I love You so much.

Secondly, I want to thank my wonderful, faithful husband and best friend, Taylor Boydston. He was the one who bought me my first Strong's Concordance, my first guitar and taught me how to search the Scriptures and how to worship Jesus. He is a true example of a man of God. My Love, I am so blessed to be your wife. Thank you for taking care of me and loving me just the way I am, I love you forever.

Table of Contents

Introduction 3
Chapter I - Fear from the Unknown 8
Chapter II - Fear of the lack of provision 11
Chapter III - Fear of the opinion and disgrace of men 17
Chapter IV - Fear/Care for your children or anybody close to you 27
Fear of not having any children 31
Chapter V - Fear of death 34
Chapter VI - Fear of inadequacy 45
Chapter VII - Being afraid of God 53
Chapter VIII - Fear of God's judgment 59
Chapter IX - Fear of the enemy 63
Chapter X - Other types of fear 70
Fear of the sufferings for righteousness sake 70
Fear of the multitudes 70
Fear from family members 71
Fear of being cursed, Fear of Idols, Demons or Other Creatures 73
Chapter XI - Discouragement 74
Chapter XII - What to do when we fear? 83
Chapter XIII - Above All... 93
Conclusion 99

Introduction

As we read the Scriptures, we see that God is constantly telling us to "Fear not." Unfortunately, the world around us is full of fear. The Bible said in 1 John 4:18, *"Fear hath* (comes with) *torment."* So many of us have been tormented with fear all our lives, but God constantly tells us, "Fear not!" because His desire is that we would be filled with His perfect love, free from fear.

First, let me start by saying this: natural fear serves a purpose, and that is to protect us. Fear can keep you from doing something that can harm you. Also, when we are afraid, our body produces adrenalin that can give us the extra strength we need to face and overcome the thing that makes us afraid. When we are afraid, we will do one of two things: either fight or flee. I believe after the fall of man (Adam & Eve), fear was created in us for our protection, by the mercy of God. Natural fear can protect us, but it also can keep us from something great. The problem with fear is that if we don't have our spiritual eyes open, we can't make a difference between real danger and the lies of the devil who wants to stop us from fullfilling God's word in our lives by intimidating us.
I believe fear was originally created as part of our human nature to protect us from anything that tries to come against us to hurt us in this natural world. Before the fall, there was no reason to fear because God gave Adam dominion over all things and the earth with all its being were under his submission. But after the fall, he lost it for a season. I believe fear is there until we allow Jesus to open our eyes and restore that authority that was initially given to us. It will happen if we die daily and we wholey submit ourselves to Him and his Word. Until that day when we are made perfect, He has given us His word that we can use it daily against the enemy, and we can be without fear. He gave us power over all the power of the enemy (Luke 10:19). We just need to believe and grow up unto it. Like it says in Galatians 4:1-4: *"¹Now I say, That the heir, as long as he is a child, differeth nothing from a servant, though he be lord of all; ²But is under tutors and governors until the time appointed of the father. ³Even so we, when we were children, were in bondage under the elements of the world: ⁴But when the fulness of the time was come, God sent forth his Son, made of a woman, made under the law."* God's perfect will is that we would be without fear and if we can see as God does, we will not fear. Like I said, fear is meant to be for our protection, but as soon the enemy recognized its power, he uses it for his advantage and use it against us.

The first time fear appeared in the Scriptures was after the fall of man. Adam and Eve had eaten from the tree of the knowledge of good and evil, and consequently, rather than going to God and trusting in Him, they found themselves running and hiding from God in fear. "Trust" in the Hebrew means: <u>to go to the right hand</u>, to flee for protection, shelter, etc. On the contrary, one of the words for "fear" means: <u>to turn aside from the road</u> (for a lodging or any other purpose), that is, sojourn (as a guest); also to shrink, <u>fear (as in a strange place)</u>; or in other words, to **turn aside from the road of God's right hand**. Fear is the very opposite of trust! Also, when we turn aside from the road to perfection, from the highway of holiness or when we quit the race that we entered into after salvation, we'll become fearful and will "fear as in a strange place". When you leave the presence of God, you'll be in a strange place and fear will arise immediately in your heart.

Adam and Eve first walked in the presence of God. It wasn't until after their fall that they began to hide themselves in fear. Once we take our eyes off of Jesus and eat from the tree of the knowledge of good and evil, we'll start reasoning within ourselves, causing doubt to arise. And as that doubt grows, it will birth fear. You see, first we sin, then we immediately forget who our God is and as a result, fear arises. That's why it's important that we get to know God intimately and stay in the Spirit. Also we ought to remember, *"Brethren, whatsoever things are true, whatsoever things are honest, whatsoever things are just, whatsoever things are pure, whatsoever things are lovely, whatsoever things are of good report; if there be any virtue, and if there be any praise, think on these things"* (Philippians 4:8).

Fear is the greatest weapon of the enemy. It is a lie and the devil is the Father of lies. He lies to you and his lies make you afraid. Therefore, whenever fear arises in our hearts, we just need to cast it down, because it's not from God. The truth is, Satan cannot really touch us, he doesn't have the power to do so, so he uses fear to keep us from Jesus and from fulfilling the call of God in our lives (Nehemiah 6:1-19). The reason why I put this study together is because I believe that we need to uncover the lies of the enemy and see God's side of this matter.

Fear is being afraid of something that MAY or MAY NOT happen in the future. But all that we really have and are really living in is the present. *"If ye then be not able to do that thing which is least, why take ye thought for the rest?"* (Luke 12:26). So don't take thought for tomorrow! What's there to fear when we don't even know what's in the future? We don't know what the future will bring; only God does. The future is not now, the future is not present and the future is subject to change. How many sleepless nights have we had due to worrying, only to wake up the next day realizing that there was really nothing to worry about? All the worst that we've imagined the previous night, doesn't even happen in the following day. Fear is just a shadow; it's not the real thing. So, what we're afraid of is nothing but a mere shadow; we fear something that's just an idea. Even if any of our worries and fears were to really happen, in the moments they do, it is no longer fear but determination to deal with the problem that overtakes us and in that God will help us. Fear is just something that the enemy uses against us and he can use it so powerfully. I know it's easier said than done, but believe me, little by little, as we get to know and trust in God more and more and let His Word wash over us, fear will decrease in our hearts; over time, the day will come when we will be completely free from fear. It is our daily warfare. We need to use the weapons that God has given us. Surely at the end we will overcome, because Jesus already overcame for us.

Jesus doesn't want us to be afraid, He wants us to trust Him. That's why He is constantly telling His people, "Fear not!" As I've pointed out earlier, the **opposite of trust is fear.** When you don't trust or have confidence in God, fear arises. For example, as shown in Numbers 14:19, Israel was constantly doubting God: *"Only rebel not ye against the LORD,* **neither fear ye** *the people of the land; for they are bread for us: their defence is departed from them, and the LORD is with us:* **fear them not**.*"* Because of their lack of faith and trust in God, Israel was constantly complaining, murmuring and in fear for their lives. They were looking upon the natural circumstances rather than in the spiritual. In other words, they were looking on the things that were seen rather than the things that were not seen. We simply need to trust in Him as David did in Psalms 56:3, *"What time I am afraid, I will trust in thee."*

Fear is very powerful and can make us do all kinds of things. And it is not only the enemy that uses fear to his advantage, but sometimes God Himself also uses fear as a tool to deal with us. He surely will if we are being so rebellious and stiffed-necked that we won't listen to anything else. Just as He uses the enemy to afflict us until we finally turn, repent and go back to Him, He can also use fear to turn us back to Him. Although God's first choice and highest way to turn us back to Him is through love, not fear, but He would do and use whatever it takes to bring us back to Him. Ezekiel 12:19 says, *"Say unto the people of the land, Thus saith the Lord God of the inhabitants of Jerusalem, and of the land of Israel; They shall eat their bread with <u>carefulness</u>* (with fear, anxiety), *and drink their water with* *astonishment, that her land may be desolate from all that is therein, because of the <u>violence</u> of all them that dwell therein.*" One definition for "Violence" in the Hebrew is: unjust gain. Here in Ezekiel, God has allowed fear to come into the lives of the Israelites as a punishment for their disobedience, or unjust gain. Fear can come when we are out of the will of God. Fear can come with His judgment. God's motivation is love, but if we won't listen after many, many times, He uses fear. He knows that in some cases, only fear can make us walk on the right path. It is only to make us better though. He loves us so much and so He would do whatever it takes to not lose us. He is longing for you and me. He is Love. He can't deny love; He cannot deny Himself. Everything He does comes out of love. That's who He is. So fear not! And believe Him; that He is able to deliver you and He is able to keep you.

If you know God's character, and that He is love, you can be sure that you're safe in His hands. **Surety brings confidence and peace** and a lack thereof can raise doubt and doubt can birth fear. Therefore, fear comes from not knowing God intimately. But again, if you know God's character and His will in every situation, then you have nothing to fear. Once you get to know Him intimately, you'll know that you always have someone who's got your back. When you know Him, you'll know that even if everybody else leaves, forsakes or betrays you, you will still have the Creator of the whole universe there for you, loving you and caring for you. As in Psalms 27:1, you can therefore say boldly and in confidence, "*The LORD is my light and my salvation; whom shall I fear? the LORD is the strength of my life; of whom shall I be afraid?*" In order that we may gain this kind of confidence for ourselves, with all our might, we need to apply our hearts to God's ways, plans and thoughts, and most especially: our relationship with Him. As we grow in Him and as we let Perfect Love (God Himself, for He *is* love) increasingly grow within us, we will be free from fear and have complete trust in Him. 1 John 4:18 seals that statement in affirming that, "*There is no fear in love; but **perfect love casteth out fear**: **because fear hath torment**. He that feareth is not made perfect in love.*" The word perfect means: complete in labor, growth, mental or moral character, completeness. We have to first grow up in agape love. It is a process, but once we've accomplished that, we'll be without fear. God is Love, and he that fears is not made perfect in God. Once we reach that perfection, we will be fearless. That's why we need to stay and sit at the feet of Jesus as Mary did, sitting under the Word of God.

When you search the Scriptures about fear, you'll find that different men and women of God struggled with different kinds of fear. On the other hand, you'll also find that many of them were actually wonderful examples of those who overcame their fear as they obeyed, served and walked with God. As we read what the Scriptures say about fear, I pray that little by little you will let the Word of God wash your heart and strengthen you and deliver you from all fears. God tells us in Leviticus 26:6, *"And I will give peace in the land, and ye shall lie down, and none shall make you afraid: and I will rid evil beasts out of the land, neither shall the sword go through your land."* This is God's promise to us.

Chapter I

Fear From the Unknown

The unknown can be scary. We can't control it and maybe that's what makes it scary. The unknown raises many questions, like: What would or what could happen? Some people, including myself, are planners and we like to be in control of our situations. We like to know things so that we can be prepared for whatever comes our way; we want to be ready for anything that could happen. That's natural because we, mankind, have eaten from the fruit of the tree of the knowledge of good and evil. **We want to know all things and if we don't, it scares us. But Christianity is about walking by faith** and not by sight. Faith can make the unseen seen! For, **"*Now faith is** the substance of things hoped for, **the <u>evidence</u> of things not seen**.*" (Hebrews 11:1)

Throughout the Scriptures, we are advised to look upon the things that are not seen, as we are told in 2 Corinthians 4:18, *"While we look not at the things which are seen, but at the things which are not seen: for the things which are seen are temporal; but the things which are not seen are eternal."* Also in 1 Samuel 16:7, *"But the LORD said unto Samuel, Look not on his countenance, or on the height of his stature; because I have refused him: for the LORD seeth not as man seeth; for man looketh on the outward appearance, but the LORD looketh on the heart."* Look not on the outward appearance, but on the unseen: the heart. Even if we can't see everything in the natural and even if we don't know what's going on, we just need to believe God and live in faith and hope. That's what He requires of us. The hope we have is not seen or else it wouldn't be hope. Romans 8:24 - *"For we are saved by hope: but hope that is seen is not hope: for what a man seeth, why doth he yet hope for?"*

The devil first tricked us to eat of the tree of the knowledge of good and evil and now he uses that to make us afraid. Our eyes were closed after the fall of man. However, we should not fear the unknown, because God doesn't want us to be blind. In James 1:5, He told us to ask for wisdom, *"If any of you lack wisdom, let him ask of God, that giveth to all men liberally, and upbraideth not; and it shall be given him."* And He also sent the Holy Ghost to guide us. So Fear not!

We don't see in the spiritual naturally, but we cannot understand Him in the natural because, as it is said in John 4:24, God is a spirit. And as 1 Corinthians 2:14 puts it plainly, *"The natural man receiveth not the things of the Spirit of God: for they are foolishness unto him: neither can he know them, because they are spiritually discerned."* Because of that, our walk is by faith. **Maybe we don't see (unless Jesus opens our eyes), but we can walk by faith.** We have the Holy Spirit within us to guide us. Jesus came to open the blind eyes and sent the Holy Spirit to help us to know the things of God, because only the Spirit of God knows the things of God, 1 Corinthians 2:10-13:

> *"¹⁰But God hath revealed them unto us by his Spirit: for the Spirit searcheth all things, yea, the deep things of God. ¹¹For what man knoweth the things of a man, save the spirit of man which is in him? even so the things of God knoweth no man, but the Spirit of God. ¹²Now we have received, not the spirit of the world, but the spirit which is of God; that we might know the things that are freely given to us of God. ¹³Which things also we speak, not in the words which man's wisdom teacheth, but which the Holy Ghost teacheth; comparing spiritual things with spiritual."*

The Holy Spirit came to guide us so that we can know and look upon the spiritual things. Once we walk after the Spirit we will know all things *"Ye have an unction from the Holy One, and ye know all things"* (1 John 2:20). Knowing the unknown begins when we are baptized in the Holy Ghost with the evidence of speaking in tongues. But again many can't receive the Spirit of God because they can't see Him: *"The Spirit of truth; whom the world cannot receive, because it seeth him not, neither knoweth him: but ye know him; for he dwelleth with you, and shall be in you"* (John 14:17).

Nebuchadnezzar was a great example of those who are afraid because he didn't have the Holy Spirit to guide him. For when he had a dream and did not understand it, he became sorely afraid, Daniel 4:5, *"I saw a dream which made me afraid, and the thoughts upon my bed and the visions of my head troubled me."*

Therefore we need to get baptized in the Holy Ghost and need to search the Scriptures, for it is given to us to know the mystery of God so that we may not be afraid of the unknown. And everything is done by faith, for without faith we can't please God (Hebrews 11:6). So, even as we can't fully understand and see ahead or beyond our present situations, we can walk by faith with the Holy Spirit.

Chapter II

Fear of the Lack of Provision

In the book of Job, Satan told God that if He were to take everything from Job, Job would curse God. Even today the devil tries to torture us by concerning us with our physical provisions. He wants us to lose our focus on God, and to do that, he distracts us with the worries and cares for our everyday natural needs. Satan wants us to be afraid of losing everything that we have. Nonetheless, God is the one in control and with authority. As shown in the book of Job, Satan had to ask permission from God before he could do anything to Job. Even now, just as before, God is always the one in control, not Satan. It is God's words that are true and eternal, and He keeps His words. For that reason, we can rest assured with confidence in Him. He said: "Be careful for nothing!"

Jesus said this of me, "You are troubled and careful about many things." Whether it is dealing with financial provision, the concerns and needs of my family members, my personal spiritual deficiencies, or with whatever it may be, I can at times get carried away in worrying about it. But God has reminded me of His assuring truths and promises considering my provision, which I will also share to you throughout this chapter, because I don't believe that I am the only one who has often times burdened myself with the worries and cares in life.

The Word of God said in Philippians 4:6, *"Be careful for nothing; but in every thing by prayer and supplication with thanksgiving let your requests be made known unto God."*

Because of the fall of man, we are, in our natural state; worrisome, fearful and careful for everything. It all started with the fall. In Genesis 3:16, God spoke to the woman, *"Unto the woman he said, I will greatly multiply thy sorrow and thy conception; in **sorrow** thou shalt bring forth children; and thy desire shall be* *to thy husband, and he shall rule over thee."* Then in verse 17, God spoke to Adam saying, *"...Because thou hast hearkened unto the voice of thy wife, and hast eaten of the tree, of which I commanded thee, saying, Thou shalt not eat of it: cursed is the ground for thy sake; in **sorrow** shalt thou eat of it all the days of thy life."*

The Hebrew definition of sorrow is: worrisomeness that is labor or pain. It comes from a root word that means: to curve, to worry pain or anger, fabricate in a bad sense. In the natural state, the women's curse is to worry and care for their children, but the men's is to be worried for their provision.

Genesis 3:19 says, *"In the **sweat of thy face** shalt thou eat bread, till thou return unto the ground; for out of it wast thou taken: for dust thou art, and unto dust shalt thou return."* Sweat in the Hebrew means: perspiration. Its root word means: agitate as with fear in the sense of sweating. Face in the Hebrew means: nose, nostril (from the rapid breathing in passion), hence the face. The man is sweating in anger, worry and fear because of the labor for provision. But it says that this will be *"**till** thou return unto the ground"*. Then God put a flaming sword which turned every way to keep the way of the tree of life (verse 24). The only way men can go back, is through the sword, which is the Word of God. The only redemption of our flesh is the Word of God, the two edged sword. The sword is the Word of God and the flaming sword is the Word of God combined with God's purging, sanctifying fire.

Jesus said *"seek ye first the kingdom of God, and his righteousness; and all these things shall be added unto you."* A big part of seeking the Kingdom of God is going through the "flaming sword" and if we do that, we can get back into the ground of Eden where we will be restored, without any worry and fear, and we can live in a place of abundance in every area of our lives. You know what really shows our Father's heart? That it is enough for Him just to see us **seek** the Kingdom of God. If you try your best to please Him, with a pure heart, He will take care of all your needs right now, even before you have completely entered in, or "found" the Kingdom of God.

But why does this happen in the first place? Genesis 3:17 say *"...thou hast **hearkened** unto the voice of thy wife, and hast eaten of the tree..."* Hearkened in the Hebrew means: to hear (with implication of obedience). He didn't just listen to Eve, but obeyed too. He rebelled against the Word of God and instead, listened to the voice of His wife. We bring fear and worry into our lives by rebelling against the Word of God. Psalms

107:11-12 says: "*Because they rebelled against the words of God, and contemned the counsel of the most High: Therefore he brought down their heart with **labour**; they fell down, and there was none to help.*" Labour in the Hebrew means: toil, that is, wearing effort; hence **worry**, whether of body or mind. Work is something that calls for hard labor, and in turn, worry. It is not on the list of the Blessings of God.

Worry also comes from the devil. It is what he uses to torment us. Psalms 10:7 - "*His mouth is full of cursing and deceit and fraud: under his tongue is **mischief** and vanity.*" Mischief is the same Hebrew word as labour found in Psalms 107:11-12.

But thank God we have Jesus, and He broke the curse. He paid the price. So He can boldly say "*Be careful for nothing; but in every thing by prayer and supplication with thanksgiving let your requests be made known unto God.*" (Philippians 4:6). We need to take this seriously. The only thing He asks us to do is to give thanks in everything, and cast all our cares upon Him because he cares for us (1 Peter 5:7), and pray to Him. That's all. I know our flesh thinks it's not enough and wants to toil and do work that brings worry, but it is so clear that He just wants us to trust in Him. We can't do it on our own anyway. He says: "*If ye then be not able to do that thing which is least, why take ye thought for the rest?*" (Luke 12:26). Isn't that liberating?

In our world if you do not care, you're labeled as someone that is not responsible. The pressure is so great. If you're not "careful" then people think something wrong with you. That's our nature. God, from the beginning, wanted us to completely trust in Him and depend on Him only. A great example of that is when He gave manna for provision. Everybody was to gather only enough for a DAY. If they gathered more, it went bad. For a day! People tried to gather more because they worried that they won't have any tomorrow, but Jesus says: "*Take therefore no thought for the morrow: for the morrow shall take thought for the things of itself. Sufficient unto the day is the evil thereof.*" (Matthew 6:34). Only once out of seven times could they gather for the next day also. You see there is no place for "saving accounts" before the 7th day. God wanted to teach them that they can trust in Him, and that they could surely depend on Him. This is what the Bible says about gathering manna: "*This is the thing which the LORD hath commanded, Gather of it every man according to his eating, an omer for every man, according to the number of your persons; take ye every man for them which are in his tents.*" (Exodus 16:16). Some people had to gather for "his people" also. They could gather more, but they had to give to those that could not go out and gather it for themselves. They were mostly children or sick people that were unable to gather manna. They were the ones *"which are in his tents"*. So if we have more than we need, it is because we need to give it to somebody who is in need in our "tents". *"As it is written, He that had gathered much had nothing over; and he that had gathered little had no lack."* (2 Corinthians 8:15) and *"But by an equality, that now at this time your abundance may be a supply for their want, that their abundance also may be a supply for your want: that there may be equality:"* (2 Corinthians 8:14)

Only before every 7th day can we gather more and put it aside. And I believe that we will have to gather more before THE 7th day also, the last day of the Lord, both in a spiritual and natural sense. Don't misunderstand me, I believe in prosperity and there are times to gather more, but what I am saying is that most of the times, 6 times out of seven, don't. So if you don't have a college fund for your kids 5 years in advance, or you don't have a huge saving account, then I say "Take no thought". But when I talk about provision I'm not just talking about finances, but spiritual, mental, and physical provision also because *"my God shall supply **ALL** your need according to his riches in glory by Christ Jesus."* (Philippians 4:19).

Again, Jesus doesn't want us to worry. The curse is broken! We don't have to live in fear. He paid the price! That's why He says it over and over again "Take no thought!"

Matthew 6:25 - *"Therefore I say unto you, **Take no thought** for your life, what ye shall eat, or what ye shall drink; nor yet for your body, what ye shall put on. Is not the life more than meat, and the body than raiment?".* In verse 27 He asks a valid question: *"Which of you by taking thought can add one cubit unto his stature?"* Another translation says: *"And who of you by worrying and being anxious can add one unit of measure to his stature or to the span of his life?"* I know it's easier to say than do, but believe me, as you search the Word of God, you get to know Him better. Then you will trust in Him more and believe that whatever He says is true and that it's enough just to let Him know about your need, worship Him, and know that He will take care of your problem. If you give it to God, you need to believe that He wants the best for you. So whatever may happen, even if it doesn't look so good, it's what is best for you, for that moment. He knows the end from the beginning, He knows you better than you know yourself. But we need to spend time in His Word. Remember that the only way to a place of no worry is back through the flaming sword. We need to give ourselves to the Word of God, and the purging fire of the Holy Spirit, and then we can live free from fear and worry. Verse 31 says again "Take no thought", verse 34: "Take no thought for tomorrow". Matthew 10:19, Luke 12:11 - *"But when they deliver you up, take no thought how or what ye shall speak"*.

Luke 12:22 - **"Take no thought** *for your life, what ye shall eat; neither for the body, what ye shall put on."* Verse 26: *" If ye then be not able to do that thing which is least, why take ye thought for the rest?"* That's what I am asking myself when worry and fear arises. Why? I can't help it, only Jesus can. So I give it to Him, I repent if I sinned, I ask for His forgiveness, I thank Him for His faithfulness and mercy, and I say *"Lord, I believe; help thou mine unbelief."* (Mark 9:24). You see, the truth is that: *"if we be dead with him, we shall also live with him: If we suffer, we shall also reign with him: if we deny him, he also will deny us:"* and after that *"**If we believe not, yet he abideth faithful: he cannot deny himself.**"* (2 Timothy 2:13).

In the Greek, the word "worry" means: to be anxious about, through the idea of distraction. We need to fight, and don't let the devil or our mind rob us and distract us from Jesus through fear and worry. Don't be like Martha, who was troubled about so many things and was distracted from the very thing that could bring her freedom from worry and fear, which is Jesus, the Living Word.

In Jeremiah 17:8 we can read this: *"For he shall be as a tree planted by the waters, and [that] spreadeth out her roots by the river, and **shall not see** when heat cometh, but her leaf shall be green; and **shall not be careful** in the year of drought, neither shall cease from yielding fruit."* And the 7th verse says this: *"Blessed [is] the man that trusteth in the Lord, and whose hope the Lord is."* The only thing God is asking from you is to trust in Him. Then you don't need to fear the time of drought because you will have the confidence that He will take care of you. There can be famine all around you; your natural mind says that is impossible, yet still, He takes care of you. It's not enough to say once that fear is the enemy of trust. If you trust God, you won't fear when "heat cometh", but those that trust in men *"shall be like the heath in the desert, and shall not see when good cometh; but shall inhabit the parched places in the wilderness, [in] a salt land and not inhabited."* (Jeremiah 17:6)

The only thing we need to do is to obey God. Do whatever He says. Give and it will be given unto you. Great example for this the widow woman who listened to Elijah and she have done all Elijah asked of her. This woman only had flour enough for one bread and Elijah asked her to make a cake out of it for him first. *"And Elijah said unto her, Fear not; go [and] do as thou hast said: but make me thereof a little cake first, and bring [it] unto me, and after make for thee and for thy son. 14 For thus saith the Lord God of Israel, The barrel of meal shall not waste, neither shall the cruse of oil fail, until the day [that] the Lord sendeth rain upon the earth. 15 And she went and did according to the saying of Elijah: and she, and he, and her house, did eat [many] days. 16 [And] the barrel of meal wasted not, neither did the cruse of oil fail, according to the word of the Lord, which he spake by Elijah."* (1 Kings 17:13-16) It doesn't sound so logical at first, still the woman obeyed the word of the Lord that came through Elijah, and she trusted God. After this she never lacked anymore. What a faithful and caring God we serve!

Finally in Psalms 46:10 God exhorts us to ***"Be still**, and know that I am God: I will be exalted among the heathen, I will be exalted in the earth."* "Be still" in the Hebrew means: stop striving, let it alone. God wants us to stop striving about our provision and just let it alone and let God to take care of it. He wants us to simply trust in Him. If we do whatever He says to us we have nothing to worry.

Let me finish by repeating what was said and asking you this: *"Which of you by taking thought can add one cubit unto his stature?" "If ye then be not able to do that thing which is least, why take ye thought for the rest?"* **so cast** *"all your care upon him; for he careth for you"* **and** *"Be careful for nothing; but in every thing by prayer and supplication with thanksgiving let your requests be made known unto God."* Hallelujah!

Chapter III

Fear of the Opinion and Disgrace of Men

Naturally we want to please men. We want men to love us. Because of that, we do or we don't do a lot of things so we won't disappoint them. Opinions of men can shape our lives if we let them. Too many people become insecure, or have a low self-esteem or don't fulfill God's calling because they listen to what people say to them through out their lifetime. But we only need to listen to what God says about us. We should not let the opinion of man alter what God said us to do or to be. Men aren't perfect, they don't know all things, but God does. Listen and obey Him. Yes, we are set under tutors and governors until the time appointed, and we need to honor them, but we should not fear the opinion of man more than God's opinion.

I. Fear not the Reproach of People!

    A. Isaiah 51:7- 8 – *"Hearken unto me, ye that know righteousness, the people in whose heart is my law;* **fear ye not the reproach of men, neither be ye afraid of their revilings.** *For the moth shall eat them up like a garment, and the worm shall eat them like wool: but my righteousness shall be for ever, and my salvation from generation to generation."*

First let us examine some of the above mentioned words:

    1. Fear (H3372) - to *fear*; morally to *revere*; causatively to *frighten* otr. (put in) fear
    2. Reproach (H2781) - *contumely*, *disgrace*, the *pudenda*
    3. Reviling (H1421) – **vilification**
    4. Afraid (H2865) - to *prostrate*; hence to **break down**, either (literally) by violence, or (figuratively) by **confusion** and fear

Fear brings confusion. Fear breaks you down. So don't break down because of their vilification! Don't break down by violence or even confusion and fear of their vilification! Read this other translation:

"Listen now, <u>*you who know right from wrong,*</u> *<u>you who hold my teaching inside you:</u> **Pay no attention to insults, and when mocked don't let it get***

you down*. Those insults and mockeries are moth-eaten, from brains that are termite-ridden, But my setting-things-right lasts, my salvation goes on and on and on."* (The Message Isaiah 51:7-8)

There is a key here: He talks to those who hold His teachings inside of them. We need to be taught of God.

    B.   Ezekiel 2:6 – *"And thou, son of man, be not afraid of them,* **neither be afraid of their words***, though briers and thorns be with thee, and thou dost dwell among scorpions:* **be not afraid of their words***, nor be dismayed at their looks, though they be a rebellious house."*

Ezekiel was afraid of the words of the rebellious people of Israel. God doesn't want fear stop you doing His will. (verse 8 *"But thou, son of man, hear what I say unto thee; Be not thou rebellious like that rebellious house: open thy mouth, and eat that I give thee."*)

    C.   Exodus 32:22-24 – *"And Aaron said, Let not the anger of my lord wax hot: thou knowest the people, that they are set on mischief. For they said unto me, Make us gods, which shall go before us: for as for this Moses, the man that brought us up out of the land of Egypt, we wot not what is become of him."* - Aaron feared men rather than God when he made the golden calf.

    D.   1 Samuel 15:24 – *"And Saul said unto Samuel, I have sinned: for I have transgressed the commandment of the LORD, and thy words: because* **I feared the people***, and obeyed their voice."* - Then in verse 20 he said *"I have sinned: yet <u>honour me now</u>, I pray thee, <u>before</u> the elders of my <u>people</u>, and before Israel, and turn again with me, that I may worship the LORD thy God."*

Saul feared the people rather than God. The opinion of men was more important to him than the opinion of God. Don't make the same mistake! When everything is done we will stand before God alone. This wasn't the first when the opinion of people moved Saul. His relationship with David was destroyed because of this. 1 Samuel 18:7-9 says, *"And the women answered one another as they played, and said, Saul hath slain his thousands, and David his ten thousands. And Saul was very wroth, and the saying displeased him; and he said, They have ascribed unto David ten thousands, and to me they have ascribed but thousands: and what can he have more but the kingdom? And <u>Saul eyed David from that day and forward</u>."* Saul loved

David until this point, but here, he was so moved by what the people said that he allowed it to ruin their relationship. When the people gave more glory to David, he couldn't look at David the same from that point on. You see what the opinion of man mixed with pride can do to you? The fear of man can separate even the closest of friends.

- E. Deuteronomy 1:28 – *"Whither shall we go up?* **our brethren have discouraged our heart, saying,** *The people is greater and taller than we; the cities are great and walled up to heaven; and moreover we have seen the sons of the Anakims there."*

Fear discourages you. The disbelief and fear of others can make you become fearful and discouraged. The word "discouraged" means (H4549) to *liquefy*; figuratively to *waste* (with disease), to *faint* (with fatigue, fear or grief) **Don't be moved by the opinion of other people! Listen to the witness in your heart!**

- F. Galatians 2:11-14 - *"*[11]*But when Peter was come to Antioch, I withstood him to the face, because he was to be blamed.* [12]*For before that certain came from James,* **he did eat with the Gentiles***: but when they were come,* **he withdrew and separated himself, fearing them which were of the circumcision***.* [13]*And the other Jews dissembled likewise with him; insomuch that* **Barnabas also was carried away with their dissimulation***.* [14]*But when I saw that they walked not uprightly according to the truth of the gospel, I said unto Peter before them all, If thou, being a Jew, livest after the manner of Gentiles, and not as do the Jews, why compellest thou the Gentiles to live as do the Jews?"*

Peter cared so much about what the Jews would say; that even though he knew better, he did what displeased God in order to please men. His sin also affected Barnabas, who followed him in this error. Our sins affect others; we shouldn't draw people away in our sins. Paul had to rebuke him.

II. Fear of the Pharisees:

- A. John 7:13 - *"Howbeit no man spake openly of him for fear of the Jews."*
- B. John 19:38 – *"And after this Joseph of Arimathaea, being a disciple of Jesus, but secretly for fear of the Jews, besought Pilate that he might take away the body of Jesus: and Pilate gave him leave. He came therefore, and took the body of Jesus."*

- C. John 20:19 – *"Then the same day at evening, being the first day of the week, when the doors were shut where the disciples were assembled for fear of the Jews, came Jesus and stood in the midst, and saith unto them, Peace be unto you."*
- D. John 9:22 - *"These words spake his parents, because they feared the Jews: for the Jews had agreed already, that if any man did confess that he was Christ, he should be put out of the synagogue."*

Many people fear the religious system.

III. Religious people are afraid of the opinion of man.

First of all let me make it clear that there is difference between a believer and religious people. Religious people follow all kinds of rules and regulations instead of God's Word and they forget about the grace and mercy of God. For example, the Pharisees made hundreds and hundreds of laws out of the original ten that God gave them. They bound their people with their traditions and man made rules and regulations. They forgot about God's grace and they listened not to the Word of God and they got so far from Him that they didn't even recognized the Messiah that they waited for so long. Don't let traditions and man made laws hardened your heart to the point that you don't even recognize Jesus anymore! Religious people fear man. We can see in the next few verses.

- A. Matthew 21:26 - *"But if we shall say, Of men;* **we fear the people**; *for all hold John as a prophet."* – This conversation was between Jesus and the high priests, and it shows the thoughts of the priests. Jesus asked them where did come from John's baptism. These priests feared men.
- B. Matthew 21:46 - *"But when they sought to lay hands on him,* **they feared the multitude**, *because they took him for a prophet."* – Here the Pharisees wanted to kill Jesus, and only the fear of men stopped them in that.
- C. Luke 22:2 - *"And the chief priests and scribes sought how they might kill him; for they feared the people."* – They wanted to kill Jesus because they were afraid of the people.
- D. Acts 5:26 - *"Then went the captain with the officers, and brought them without violence: for* **they feared the people**, *lest they should have been stoned."* – The apostles escaped from prison with the help of God's angels and they went to preach in the temple. Once the Pharisees have heard about it, they sent for them, but since they feared the people thy did that without violence.

Religious people fear people. I mean it's great that they didn't touch John or Jesus before His time because they were afraid, but the true motivation should be the fear of God and not of man. That's what religion does. The opinion of people is so important to them that they mingle the Word of God with whatever men want to hear so they can please them. 2 Timothy 4:3-4 *"³**For the time will come when they will not endure sound doctrine; but after their own lusts shall they heap to themselves teachers, having itching ears;** ⁴And they **shall turn away** their ears **from the truth**, and shall be turned unto fables."*

The Laodicean church in the book of Revelation speaks of the church in the last days, and the word Laodicea means: opinion of the people, the rule of the people, majority. It's no longer what God wants first, but what the people want. The fear of men and the fear of the opinion of men is really dangerous because it puts man on the throne rather than God. We can't serve two master. We need to make a decision that we listen to God or man.

    E.   Matthew 14:5 - *"And when he would have put him to death, **he feared the multitude**, because they counted him as a prophet."* - Herod feared people rather than God.

IV.   This is how David prayed when he feared men's reproach:

    A.   Psalms 119:22, 31, 39 – *"**Remove from me reproach** and contempt; for I have kept thy testimonies…I have stuck unto thy testimonies: O LORD, put me not to shame… **Turn away my reproach which I fear**: for thy judgments are good."*

Reproach in the Hebrew means: fear from scorn, disgrace, shame, reproach, being exposed

    B.   Psalms 39:8 - *"Deliver me from all my transgressions: **make me not the reproach of the foolish.**"*

V.   This is what God said about the fear of man and the opinion of man:

    A.   Deuteronomy 1:17 – *"Ye shall **not respect persons in judgment**; but ye shall hear the small as well as the great; **ye shall not be afraid of the face of man**; for the judgment is God's: and the cause that is too hard for you, bring it unto me, and I will hear it."*

- B. Proverbs 29:25 – *"The **fear of man bringeth a snare**: but whoso putteth his trust in the LORD shall be safe."* Fear (H2731) comes from H2730 and it means fear anxiety
- C. Jeremiah 1:8 – *"**Be not afraid of their faces**: for I am with thee to deliver thee, saith the LORD."*
- D. Jeremiah 1:17-19 – *"Thou therefore gird up thy loins, and arise, and speak unto them all that I command thee: **be not dismayed at their faces**, lest I confound thee before them... And they shall fight against thee; but they shall not prevail against thee; for I am with thee, saith the LORD, to deliver thee."* - Jeremiah was afraid of Israel, the faces of his own people.
- E. Psalms 118:8-9 - *"**It is better to trust in the LORD than to put confidence in man**. It is better to trust in the LORD than to put confidence in princes."*
- F. Jeremiah 39:17 – *"But I will deliver thee in that day, saith the LORD: and thou shalt not be given into the hand of **the men of whom thou art afraid**."*

Respecting men and men's opinion above God's is not a wise decision. We need to trust in God and look not upon the faces of men. **We need to care about what God thinks about us, and not the opinion of men.** Consider Peter: He denied Jesus; he feared men rather than trusting in God. It is hard not to be moved by people. Most of us naturally want to please man, but the truth is if we are secure in ourselves and we know who we are in God and what is the hope of our calling we will not be moved by the opinion of man. If we know the God we believe in, then there is no one who can make us afraid.

VI. <u>This was Paul advice on this subject:</u>

- A. Hebrews 13:5-6 - *"⁵**Let your conversation be without covetousness; and be content with such things as ye have**: for he hath said, I will never leave thee, nor forsake thee. ⁶<u>**So that** we may boldly say, **The Lord is my helper**, and **I will not fear what man shall do unto me**.</u>"*

If our lifestyle is without covetousness and if we are content with whatever God gives us, believing that He will never leave us or forsake us and that He is our helper, then we have nothing to fear. We need to remember this; because God is greater than man therefore, what can men can do unto us. If we do our part He is more than willing to do His.

VII. Jesus was a great example of this:

Mark 12:12-16 - "*¹²And* **they sought to lay hold on him, but feared the people**: *for they knew that he had spoken the parable against them: and they left him, and went their way. ¹³And they send unto him certain of the Pharisees and of the Herodians, to catch him in his words. ¹⁴And when they were come, they say unto him, Master, we know that thou art true, and* **carest for no man: for thou regardest not the person of men, but teachest the way of God in truth***: Is it lawful to give tribute to Caesar, or not? ¹⁵Shall we give, or shall we not give? But he, knowing their hypocrisy, said unto them, Why tempt ye me? bring me a penny, that I may see it. ¹⁶And they brought it. And he saith unto them, Whose is this image and superscription? And they said unto him, Caesar's.*"

No matter what people think or what they might do, He taught the way of God in truth. We must do the same, and not be moved with fear. We need to know who we are in God if we don't want to be moved by the opinions of people anymore. So let me share this with you what God gave me, years ago about insecurity. I hope it will bless you.

Growing up I was never really established or ensured that I was valuable or special in any way. Let me note this though I am certianly greatful for my parents. They worked hard to provide for me and my syblings and they created a safe place to live in, only they didn't give much encouragement which made me an insecure person in my heart and I spent my whole life trying to disprove that deceiving, whispering voice in my heart that told me I wasn't really good in anything I did.
So, every time I failed in something, I took it as a confirmation of that voice that said I'm not really good enough to reach great things in my life. Every little fall wasn't just a fall, but an evidence that I'm foolish just to think I could be anything. And I know we are nothing, but we also need to know that we are the apple of God's eyes and we are His precious creation. We are precious to Him, otherwise He wouldn't give His only begotten Son for us. We need to honor His sacrifice and realize that even though we are nothing, we are still precious. We can't win the battle against the enemy if we think we are nothing. Yes, compared to God, we are nothing, but compared to all of His creation, we are somebody, He has chosen us. We need to have confidence. There is a difference between being prideful and knowing who we are in God.

You know, you can easily misinterpret an insecure person and think he or she is prideful. Some may say they care too much about what people say because they are prideful. I say that they care too much about what people say, because they have such a tormenting war in their soul that says "You are nothing!" and they think that only a good feedback from man can reprove that. They know it's wrong, but sometimes they can't help it. Man's opinion is just a tool of the enemy in that stupid, inward war. It's a tool, and a decisive factor, letting them know whether they are really nothing or they are ok. Every time when they fall before men's eyes or even in their own eyes, they are starting to believe that voice. This war is really tiring. Insecurity is hard to deal with. Sometimes it takes a long time.

Many insecure people become perfectionists because they want to secure themselves from failing. Failing for an insecure person is a bigger deal than it is to others. It is a confirmation for them that they're not worthy. Again, I want you to know that I know we are nothing apart from the grace and goodness of God, but at the same time we can't clothe ourselves with false humility either. (Did you know that the Pharisees missed out because of their false humility? Acts 13:46 – *"Then Paul and Barnabas waxed bold, and said, It was necessary that the word of God should first have been spoken to you: but seeing ye put it from you, and <u>judge yourselves unworthy</u> of everlasting life, lo, we turn to the Gentiles."*) We must have a healthy balance! We ARE valuable!

An insecure person is many times accused that of thinking more highly of her or himself than they ought to think. On the contrary, they judge themselves harder than anybody else. They can come off like "holier than thou" but it's just a fruit of their inward battle. They also can become more judgmental towards others (which is not right), because they are judging themselves harder. It's a constant battle to conquer the voice that says "You are not good enough". It's exhausting, and it's not easy to overcome, but it can be done with Jesus! You see, insecure Christians have the worst time, because when they finally start to feel good about themselves, they get condemned about it, because they want to be humble. It's just a hard work to find the balance! But with Jesus, it is possible.

So what do we need to do? Just let the Word of God wash you, establish who you are in God, and teach you that failure is not the proof of your value. All of us fail, every man fails because we became like this after the "fall". But what makes us valuable is what we do after we fail. Are we dwelling in it, having pity party, or are we getting up and learning from it, not fearing any man or even our inward man, but trusting in God.

He loves you, and you are special to Him. You are not any less than any of His other creation. Maybe you are different, but different is good. There are many kinds of people with different needs, so all of us have different strengths and weakness, therefore don't look upon others because they are not you. God has a special place and position in His great plan reserved just for you. And no one can fill that place but you!

We need to judge ourselves after the Word of God and not after what we can or cannot do. What God has spoken to YOU? Are you acting on that?

And the other thing is that: God will never condemn you! So if you feel condemnation coming upon you, you have to cast it away immediately, because condemnation is not from God. Why would you entertain that condemning thought even for a minute? If you made a mistake, just repent before God, make it right with your brethren if necessary, and then you are done. What else can you do? Jesus said in Luke 12:26 – *"If ye then be not able to do that thing which is least, why take ye thought for the rest?"* Why? Forget about it! Philippians 4:6 says *"Be careful for nothing; but in every thing by prayer and supplication with thanksgiving let your requests be made known unto God."* Just worship and pray to God, give it to Him. It is finished. The day will come when it'll be easier.

We need to face the fact that we'll make a million mistakes and we'll disappoint many people, but that's not what grades us! We just need to understand that failure is going to be a part of our lives until we reach perfection. We have to focus on how we use our failures, what we do after we fail and what we can learn from it. We need to remember how God comforted us when we failed so we can comfort others with the same comfort. (2 Corinthians 1:4) How can we comfort others if we have never been comforted? How could any one comfort us if we never been in the situation when we needed comfort?

Insecurity is a lie of the devil, and it is irrational and it can be defeated by God and by His Spirit and by His Word. *"Not by might, not by power, but by my Spirit sayeth the Lord."* Don't be discouraged, sometime it'll take time but God will finish it. He said *"I will not leave thee, until I have done that which I have spoken to thee of."*

Insecurity is just a fear, a fear that we are not good enough. Fear is just a shadow; fear is not a real thing! Let me tell you; you are good enough! Jesus created you, called you made you His sons and daughters. If you are good enough for Jesus then who cares about the rest. He is the Creator of all things and He is the King of kings, the Most Holy being, so why would you rather listen to that lying voice in your head?

You are not supposed to be like others. You are fearfully and wonderfully made by Him, by the Perfection of Beauty! And about failing; **you need to accept it, that you will fall a lot before you learn how to walk. So don't avoid walking because you are afraid of failing.** And don't beat yourself up, when you fall. It's a part of learning to stay on your feet.

It's not just okay to fall, but in our present state it is necessary. It's a must. Why? Because it humbles us, it shows us that we can't do anything and we are incapable of anything apart from the grace of God. It teaches us to comfort others. It teaches us that we can and need to trust in Him because He always comes through, and makes us see His unconditional love and that He is the unconditionally loving God.

You see, before the fall, Adam and Eve were perfect, but they didn't know the unconditionally loving God. They didn't know unconditional love. Why? Because how does He show His love towards us? *"...God commendeth his love toward us, in that, while we were yet sinners, Christ died for us."* (Romans 5:8), "Commendeth" in the Greek means: to introduce, to exhibit. I believe that Adam didn't recognize God's unconditional love before his fall. How could he know that God loved him no matter what, if he had never done anything that would make him unworthy of God's love? He shows His love toward us in that; while we were yet (still) sinners, Christ died for us. God's love was introduced to man after the fall, by Jesus' sacrifice and without knowing and experiencing this love, we can't love. *"Wherefore I say unto thee, her sins, which are many, are forgiven; for she loved much: but to whom little is forgiven, the same loveth little."* (Luke 7:47). This being said, how much did Adam experience love before the fall? God is love. Adam was perfect, but was he like God? God is love. So God uses even our failing to teach, so be encouraged! I'm not saying we need to look for it either, but we need to accept the fact that if failure happens, it can teach us and can make us something greater.

Let me finish with this, Proverbs 24:16 says, *"For a just man falleth seven times, and riseth up again..."* A JUST man falleth. A JUST. Failure doesn't make you less valuable. It doesn't make you a failure. So don't give up because there is an end of failing as we see in Job 5:19- *"He shall deliver thee in six troubles: yea, in seven there shall no evil touch thee."* Hallelujah! The day will come, the seventh day when nothing can move us anymore. Thank you my wonderful Jesus for loving me for who I am! Thank you for delighting in me! I love you so much! You're the Everlasting God!"

Chapter IV

Fear/Care For Your Children or Anybody Close to You

God will take care of our children and loved ones. He doesn't want us to be afraid of losing them. His eyes are on them. We have to give them completely to Him just like Moses' mother gave her son to God's hands. When Moses' mother feared for the life of her son she put him in a little ark and put it in the river by trusting God. She had complete trust in God. God only asks us to trust and believe Him and walk with Him with all our might. Even if it happens what we feared the most, the best thing we can do is to trust in His wisdom instead of giving ourselves to even more fear. Sometimes God allows things in His wisdom that He could prevent in His power. If what we feared the most actually happens, then He will gives us the grace to deal with it, and we can rest a sure that it happened for our own good, even if we don't understand it now. Giving into fear will just make us lose our peace and break us down, bring confusion, and then simply make us sin and lead us away from the "way". We can't give into fear! Fear is destructive.
Jesus holds the key of the life and death in His hands. He's in charge. If we give ourselves to fear, we will lose our peace and get confused, then it leads us to sin and away the right hand of God (like I mentioned before in the introduction).

Let's take a moment to look at the story of Abraham. He so longed for a son and he waited so long and finally, after so much hardship, he recieved a son. Isaac was so precious to him. Many times we fear that we might lose something or somebody that is very precious to us and it's understandable, but it's still not God's will for us. His grace is sufficient for us (2 Corinthians 12:9). He knows how much we can handle and He will never allow anything in our lives that He knows we can not handle through His great grace. Grace means divine enablement. If we need to go through something that seems too great to handle, He will give us the divine enablment to be able to do it. You see, we definately will go through hard times, with a journey that seems too great at times (1 Kings 19:7), but He will give you the provision you need to make it through. Don't forget; Jesus interceeds for us so we will not fail (Luke 22:32). Sometimes He conceals a lot of things from us so we won't fear. Jeremiah said *you deceived me and I was deceived* (Jeremiah 20:7). Jesus didn't tell him everything in advance, just as much as as he could handle at the moment. Fear makes you worry about things that God already made a provision for. Fear paints the picture darker then it actually is. There is no reason to fear because even if that thing you fear comes to pass, you'll have the divine strength to handle it, and you can be assured that *the end of the thing is better than the beginning thereof* (Ecclesiastes 7:8). Jesus wouldnt just take something away from you just to hurt you. We need to undertand that. He knows our heart, He knows what we can handle, and He knows our end. So be encouraged God writes the end of all story. Many times the seemingly "bad" things that happen to you are actually orcastrated by God. You didn't even see it coming because God hid it from you and just as you were able to bear it, He revealed it to you. Why? Because He doesn't want fear to stop you from fulfilling the Word of God in your life. He doesn't want you to be tormented because you are not yet able to see through His eyes.

Many things happened in my life that, if I would have known about them in the beginning, I would have lived in fear, or would have tried to do everyting in my power just to change them so they wouldnt happen to me. They seemed so big that I would not have believed that I could have handled it once it happened. But when the time came, I had such a grace of God on me, that, although it was hard, somehow I was able bear it, and now I can see the fruit that came out of it.

Fear is often times unnecesearly. Do you hear whispers that fill you with fear? That's only your soulish nature or the devil and NOT God. And if it's not God, then why would you listen? Paul said: *Be careful for nothing!* and Jesus says that: *If ye then be not able to do that thing which is least, why take ye thought for the rest?"*

It is a constant war within our members. Genesis 25:22 – *"And the children struggled together within her... Two nations are in thy womb, and two manner of people shall be separated from thy bowels; and the one people shall be stronger than the other people; and the elder shall serve the younger."* There are two "manner of people" warring in us, but we need to fight, we need to make our souls praise God, we need to think on those things that are above, and those things that are first pure and peaceable.

Consider these words: *"**Be careful for nothing**; but in every thing by prayer and supplication with thanksgiving let your requests be made known unto God. And the peace of God, which passeth all understanding, shall keep your hearts and minds through Christ Jesus. **Finally, brethren, whatsoever things are true**, whatsoever things are **honest**, whatsoever things are **just**, whatsoever things are **pure**, whatsoever things are **lovely**, whatsoever things are **of good report**; if there **be any virtue**, and if there **be any praise, think on these things. Those things**, which ye have both **learned, and received, and heard, and seen in me, do: and the God of peace shall be with you.**"* So, to have the peace of God in us, we need to take control of our minds and think on the things above. It's not easy, and it takes time to train our mind, but every time we worry or fear tries to sneak up on us, just start quoting scriptures aloud or in your mind. Start thinking upon the things that God promises you in His word the things that give Glory to God. Be careful for nothing!

Abraham believed that God would resurrect Isaac. Abraham had no fear because he truly knew God. He knew His character, he knew that if he just obeyed God, then everything would be alright. He had no fear of losing his only God given son. Surely the situation didn't seem very good but he knew better. He knew that Jesus never changes His word and He would never ask him to do anything if the end of it wouldn't be better than the beginning thereof. Having complete trust in God makes fear flee from us. Do you know and believe the goodness of God in the land of living; In your land? (Psalms 27:13)

I. Fear/Care For Your Children or Anybody Close to You

    A. Luke 8:49-50 (Mark 5:35-36) – *"...Thy daughter is dead; trouble not the Master. But when Jesus heard it, he answered him, saying,* **Fear not: believe only, and she shall be made whole**.*"*

Jairus, a ruler of the synagogue was afraid when he received a report from his house that his daughter was dead. But Jesus immediately said fear not, believe only and He healed his daughter. So that's all we are supposed to do. Fear not and believe and trust in God. We just need to listen to God. If He said she will be all right, then there is nothing to add to it and there is nothing to fear.

    B. Genesis 21:17 - *"And God heard the voice of the lad; and the angel of God called to Hagar out of heaven, and said unto her, What aileth thee, Hagar?* ***fear not; for God hath heard the voice of the lad where he is.****"*

Hagar was afraid that she lost her son. God's eyes are on your children, He always knows where they are and what they are doing and He takes care of them even if you make mistakes.

    C. Deuteronomy 9:19 – *"For I was afraid of the anger and hot displeasure, wherewith the LORD was wroth against you to destroy you. But the LORD hearkened unto me at that time also."*

Moses feared for Israel, **He feared that God would judge them**, but he prayed to God for them, and God listened to the earnest prayers of His saint.

    D. Paul cared for all of His disciples. He loved them dearly as his own flesh and blood and he feared for their lives and states.

        1. 2 Corinthians 11:3 - *"But **I fear**, lest by any means, as the serpent beguiled Eve through his subtilty, so **your minds should be corrupted** from the simplicity that is in Christ."*

        2. 2 Corinthians 12:20 - *"For **I fear, lest, when I come, I shall not find you such as I would**, and that I shall be found unto you such as ye would not: lest there be debates, envyings, wraths, strifes, backbitings, whisperings, swellings, tumults:"*

        3. Galatians 4:11 - ***"I am afraid of you, lest I have bestowed upon you labour in vain."***

    E. Matthew 2:22 - *"But when he heard that Archelaus did reign in Judaea in the room of his father Herod, **he was afraid to go thither**: notwithstanding, being warned of God in a dream, he turned aside into the parts of Galilee."*

Joseph feared for Jesus' life. We always have to have peace in our hearts or a witness when God asks us to do something. The lack of peace can be a sign that we need to turn to God again for instruction before we do anything in that situation. God always gives us direction for what we should do in those times, so we need not to fear anymore. God warned Joseph, and he went to Nazareth. And that was the plan from the beginning Matthew 2:23 - *"And he came and dwelt in a city called Nazareth: **that it might be fulfilled which was spoken by the prophets, He shall be called a Nazarene**."* There are no coincidences in God. God uses fear, lack of peace as a sign that something is not right, but this doesn't mean that God wants us to live in fear. As soon as fear arises in our hearts we need to examine it . Is it come from the devil or is it just a lack of peace? Its like a physical pain is a sign for something wrong in our body, just like the lack of peace can fear could be an indicator for something. Therefore we need to examine it and need to treat the root of the problem. And if we do that then the symptoms are will disappear too. Just like that with fear. Fear is only a sign. Find the root of it and take care of it. The treatment is simple. Turn to God and obey to His words.

II. **Fear of not having any children**

There are so many men and women of God in the Scriptures that were barren for a season but later received a child in God's timing. God makes everything beautiful in His time. For example: Abraham and Sarah had to wait until they were around 100 years old. God wants us to be fruitful, but most of all He always wants the best for us. Sometimes the best might be not having any children, but then He also gives the grace for that. They have nothing to fear, they can rest assured if they walk with God and obey His words, God will reward them for their sacrifice. We need to trust Him; He knows the end from the beginning. We could never go wrong by trusting in His wisdom.

So here are some examples of God's faithfulness. If God said you'll have a child, and that's your heart desire, nothing can hinder that word. He said it and He will do it.

> A. Genesis 15:1-4 - *"¹After these things the word of the LORD came unto Abram in a vision, saying, **Fear not, Abram**: I am thy shield, and thy exceeding great reward. ²And Abram said, Lord GOD, what wilt thou give me, seeing I go childless, and the steward of my house is this Eliezer of Damascus? ³And Abram said, **Behold, to me thou hast given no seed**: and, lo, one born in my house is mine heir. ⁴And, behold, the **word of the LORD came unto him**, saying, This shall not be thine heir; but he **that shall come forth out of thine own bowels shall be thine heir**."*

Abraham was afraid that he wouldn't have any children and that he wouldn't have an heir that he could pass all that he had down, to someone who would also carry his name on.

There are many other examples, like Samson's mother, Rachel, Hanna etc. who were barren for a long time before God opened their womb and gave them a child. Nevertheless God's word never fails. He always gives us our heart's desire, if we love Him and if we are with Him and obey Him and His commandments.

> B. Luke 1:11-13 *"¹¹And there appeared unto him an angel of the Lord standing on the right side of the altar of incense. ¹²And when Zacharias saw him, **he was troubled, and fear fell upon him**. ¹³But the angel said unto him, **Fear not, Zacharias: for thy prayer is heard**; and thy wife **Elisabeth shall bear thee a son**, and thou shalt call his name John."*

III. This is what God said about barrenness:

A. Psalms 113:9 - "**He maketh the barren woman** to keep house, and **to be a joyful mother of children**. Praise ye the LORD."

B. Song of Solomon 4:2 - "Thy teeth are like a flock of sheep that are even shorn, which came up from the washing; whereof every one bear twins, and **none is barren among them**." - Jesus' bride won't be barren.

C. Isaiah 54:1 - "**Sing, O barren**, thou that didst not bear; break forth into singing, and cry aloud, thou that didst not travail with child: **for more are the children of the desolate** than the children of the married wife, **saith the LORD**."

Obviously these are don't only speak of natural bareness but also spiritual one. And even if you don't have any natural children at all Jesus will give you spiritual children if you're walking with Him with all your might, because just like I said that God's bride won't be barren. But in this part of the book I'm talking about bareness in the natural sense and we can apply the Word of God in the natural sense also because the Word of God "*life unto those that find them, and health to all their flesh*" (Proverbs 4:22). "All their flesh" not just for our soul. And we could have another chapter about spiritual unfruitfulness but here I just wanted to stick to fear of natural bareness.

Let me say this also. I know it's not easy to wait on God, but it worth it, I can promise you. You don't want to make the same mistake like Abraham did. God promised him a son but as time went by they started reasoning. He and his wife thought that maybe they need to do something about it rather just sit and wait for God's promise to come to pass. It is really important that whatever we do, we move on the Word of God. If He asks us to wait or if He gave us a promise then said nothing, the best thing we can do that wait on Him. Wait on His word. He will tell you when He needs you to do something. Until then just wait. I know it's not easy but it is necessary, it is a must. We need to learn Abraham and Sarah's mistake. They couldn't wait on God therefore Ishmael was born. God's promise was Isaac and not Ishmael. They could have been saved from such a heartache if they just would have wait on God. Let us trust Him and wait on Him. Psalms 37:4 says, "*Delight thyself also in the Lord; and he shall give thee the desires of thine heart.*" This is His requirement.

We also need to know that God does everything for a reason. If we follow Him, we can be sure that He always does what is best for us, even if it doesn't seem joyous in the moment, because the Bible also says Luke 23:29 - *"For, behold, the days are coming, in the which they shall say,* **Blessed are the barren, and the wombs that never bare***, and the paps which never gave suck."* Everything is about timing. There will be a time when it is better for those that are barren. Ecclesiastes 3:1 - *"To every thing there is a season, and a time to every purpose under the heaven:"* We just need to make sure that we are in the will of God and all things will work for good and we have nothing to fear.

Chapter V

Fear of Death

The enemy really likes to threaten us with loosing our lives. Satan said it in Job 2:4 *"Skin for skin, yea, all that a man hath will he give for his life."* No wonder he still tries to take our lives. But the truth is that the keys of death are in Jesus' hands (Rev. 1:18). Satan has no power over our lives. Satan can't do anything without permit from God. God has the power in His hands. We can see in Job's case that Satan had to ask permission from God before he had done anything in Job's life. God will allow some things in His wisdom that He could prevent in His power. He allowed Satan to take everything from Job except his life. We can rest assured though if we walk with God, the end of the thing will be better than the beginning thereof in every time, even if it hurts in the present.

In this chapter we take a look at how God's people reacted when their life was in danger, and we will see what God said when they were afraid of losing their lives. God doesn't want us to fear death. Death is not the end of everything, matter of fact that it could be the beginning of some wonderful thing if we obey His Word in our lives.

I.   Examples for fear of death in God's people

    A.   Abraham

        1.   Genesis 12:11-13 – *"And it came to pass, when he was come near to enter into Egypt, that he said unto Sarai his wife, Behold now, I know that thou art a fair woman to look upon: Therefore it shall come to pass, when the Egyptians shall see thee, that they shall say, This is his wife: and they will kill me, but they will save thee alive. Say, I pray thee, thou art my sister:* **that it may be well with me for thy sake**; *and* **my soul shall live** *because of thee."*

Abraham was afraid that he will lose his life for his wife's sake, and this made him lie. (Genesis 20:11 – *"And Abraham said, Because* **I thought***, Surely the fear of God is not in this place; and they will slay me for my wife's sake."*) See what fear does? He only **thought** that they will kill him. It was only just a thought in his head and it caused him to react. If we read further we can see that he only had to trust in God because He didn't let anything to happen to him. He had no reason to fear.

B. Isaac

   1. Genesis 26:7 – *"And the men of the place asked him of his wife; and he said, She is my sister: for **he feared to say, She is my wife**; lest, said he, the men of the place should kill me for Rebekah; because she was fair to look upon."*

Like father like son. Isaac feared the same thing as his father did. Isaac made the same mistake his father did. Sometimes God ask us to be crafty, like Mathew 10:16 says, *"be ye therefore wise as serpents, and harmless as doves."* But **there is a difference between craftiness and lying, and that is; the motivation of the heart. We need to ask why we do it. Are you crafty because you are obeying God's voice, or are you lying because you are afraid?** Lying out of fear is not from God, it is simply the evidence that we don't trust God and that we try to take matters into our own hands. Jesus said "Fear not; believe only" (Luke 8:50)

C. David

   1. Psalms 55:4 – *"My heart is sore pained within me: and the **terrors of death** are fallen upon me."* - "Terror" = fright, fear.
   2. Psalms 31:13-15 *"¹³For I have heard the slander of many: **fear was on every side:** while they took counsel together against me, **they devised to take away my life**. ¹⁴**But I trusted in thee, O LORD**: I said, Thou art my God. ¹⁵**My times are in thy hand**: deliver me from the hand of mine enemies, and from them that persecute me."*

David feared for his life, but his reaction was to trust in God because he knew that his seasons of life, his "times" were in God's hands. Nobody could take his life unless it was God's will. His life was in God's hands. Our lives are in His hands, so we don't need to fear those who want to kill our body, but rather, fear God.

D. The men on the boat with Paul and the disciples of Jesus

   1. Acts 27:22-24 *"²²And now I exhort you to **be of good cheer: for there shall be no loss of any man's life** among you, but of the ship. ²³For there stood by me this night the angel of God, whose I am, and whom I serve, ²⁴**Saying, Fear not, Paul; thou must be brought before***

> *Caesar: and, lo, God hath given thee all them that sail with thee."*

It doesn't matter how it appears in the natural, if God said something, then nothing can stop it. Just like when Jesus said to His disciples to go over to the other side. Then a great storm arose, but it didn't matter because God said they will go to the other side. So we just need to stand on God's word because it is eternal and permanent and it will come to pass, we can rest assure.

    2.   Mark 4:35-41 *"³⁵And the same day, when the even was come, he saith unto them,* **Let us pass over unto the other side***....³⁷And* **there arose a great storm of wind, and the waves beat into the ship***, so that it was now full. ³⁸ And he was in the hinder part of the ship, asleep on a pillow: and they awake him, and say unto him,* **Master, carest thou not that we perish?** *³⁹And he arose, and rebuked the wind, and said unto the sea, Peace, be still. And the wind ceased, and there was a great calm. ⁴⁰****And he said unto them, Why are ye so fearful? how is it that ye have no faith?*** *⁴¹And they feared exceedingly, and said one to another, What manner of man is this, that even the wind and the sea obey him?"*

        a.   Luke 8:24-25 – *"And they came to him, and awoke him, saying,* **Master, master, we perish.** *Then he arose, and* **rebuked the wind** *and the raging of the water:* **and they ceased, and there was a calm***. 25And he said unto them, Where is your faith? And they being afraid wondered, saying one to another, What manner of man is this! for he commandeth even the winds and water, and they obey him."*

First the disciples were afraid that they would lose their lives, and then they were afraid of Jesus, seeing what a powerful man He is. The only fear He wants us to have is a reverential kind of fear toward Him.

  E.   Peter

    1.   Matthew 14:30-31 - *"³⁰But* **when he saw the wind boisterous, he was afraid***; and beginning to sink, he cried, saying, Lord, save me. ³¹****And immediately Jesus stretched***

forth his hand*, and caught him, and said unto him, O thou of little faith, wherefore didst thou doubt?"*

God doesn't want us to fear death. As a matter affect, He died so we wouldn't be in bondage to death (Hebrews 2:15 *"And deliver them who through fear of death were all their lifetime subject to bondage."*)

II. The enemy, religion, and Pharisees will seek to kill you if you share the Gospel

The enemy tried to destroy those who shared Jesus and the Gospel because they themselves were afraid of them. Their motivation was fear. Our motivation should be love, trust and respect of God. We know that Jesus *"carest for no man: for thou regardest not the person of men, but teachest the way of God in truth"* (Mark 12:14). We need to do the same. We shouldn't stop teaching the truth because we fear people or fear death.

Jesus encouraged His disciple not to be afraid to preach the Gospel, because none of those leaders could touch them unless our Father let them. He cares for us, and His eyes are upon the faithful. Just like in Job's case. Satan went before God and asked permission to deal with Job, and God told him what he could or could not do. If God allows something to Satan, we can rest assure that the end of that thing will be better than the beginning thereof. Consider the end of Job. He received the double portion. James 5:11 says the following about those that endure all that God allows in their lives: *"Behold, we count them happy which endure. Ye have heard of the patience of Job, and have seen the end of the Lord; that the Lord is very pitiful, and of tender mercy."*

    A.   Matthew 10:25, 26-31 – *"…If they have called the master of the house Beelzebub, how much more shall they call them of his household?* ***Fear them not therefore****: for there is nothing covered, that shall not be revealed; and hid, that shall not be known.* ***What I tell you in darkness, that speak ye in light****: and what ye hear in the ear,* ***that preach ye upon the housetops****. And* ***fear not them which kill the body****, but are not able to kill the soul: but rather fear him which is able to destroy both soul and body in hell. Are not two sparrows sold for a farthing? and one of them shall not fall on the ground without your Father. But* ***the very hairs of your head are all numbered. Fear ye not*** *therefore, ye are of more value than many sparrows."*

    B.   Luke 12:3-5 - *"³Therefore whatsoever ye have spoken in darkness shall be heard in the light; and that which ye have spoken in the ear* in closets shall be proclaimed upon the housetops. ⁴*And I say unto you my friends,* **Be not afraid of them that kill the body,** *and after that have no more that they can do.* ⁵*But I will forewarn you whom ye shall fear:* **Fear him, which after he hath killed hath power to cast into hell**; *yea, I say unto you, Fear him."*

C. Mark 11:18 - *"And the scribes and chief priests heard it, and* **sought how they might destroy him: for they feared him**, *because all the people was astonished at his doctrine."*

III. This is how Jesus encouraged His disciples

Jesus said in Revelation 2:9-10 - *"⁹I know thy works, and tribulation, and poverty, (but thou art rich) and I know the blasphemy of them which say they are Jews, and are not, but are the synagogue of Satan.* ¹⁰**Fear none of those things which thou shalt suffer**: *behold, the devil shall cast some of you into prison, that ye may be tried; and ye shall have tribulation ten days:* **be thou faithful unto death, and I will give thee a crown of life**.*"* And also 1 Peter encourages us, *"And* **who is he that will harm you, if ye be followers of that which is good**? **But** *and if ye suffer for righteousness' sake, happy are ye: and be not afraid of their terror,* **neither be troubled**; *But sanctify the Lord God in your hearts: and be ready always to give an answer to every man that asketh you a reason of the hope that is in you with meekness and fear:"* (1 Peter 3:13-15)

IV. The Scriptures give us great examples of those that, in spite of the fear of death, preached Jesus and obeyed God

    A. Jesus

        1. John 5:18 - *"Therefore the* **Jews sought the more to kill him**, *because he not only had broken the sabbath, but* **said also that God was his Father**, *making himself equal with God."*

        2. Luke 22:2 - *"And the chief priests and scribes sought how they might kill him; for they feared the people."*

They tried to stop even Jesus, but nothing could stop Jesus from speaking about the Father and healing the sick, and see no one could touch Him until He, himself, let it by laying His life down. Nobody could do anything to Jesus until He laid down His own life; Matthew 21:46 - *"But* **when they sought to lay hands on him, they feared the multitude**, *because they took him for a prophet."*

Nobody can touch you either if you do what God commands you to do. Nobody can hurt you without God's permission so fear not, only believe!

   B.   Peter

        1.   Acts 5:28-29 - *"²⁸Saying, Did not we straitly command you that **ye should not teach in this name**? and, behold, ye have filled Jerusalem with your doctrine, and intend to bring this man's blood upon us. ²⁹Then Peter and the other apostles answered and said, **We ought to obey God rather than men**."*

   C.   Daniel

        1.   Daniel 6:7, 10 - *"All the presidents of the kingdom, the governors, and the princes, the counsellors, and the captains, have **consulted together to establish a royal statute**, and to make a firm decree, that **whosoever shall ask a petition of any God or man for thirty days**, save of thee, O king, he **shall be cast into the den of lions**... Now when **Daniel** knew that the writing was signed, he went into his house; and his windows being open in his chamber toward Jerusalem, **he kneeled upon his knees three times a day, and prayed, and gave thanks before his God, as he did aforetime**."*

            Daniel 6:16, 21-22 - *"²¹Then the king commanded, and they brought Daniel, and cast him into the den of lions. Now the king spake and said unto Daniel, Thy God whom thou servest continually, he will deliver thee...Then said Daniel unto the king, O king, live for ever. ²²**My God hath sent his angel, and hath shut the lions' mouths, that they have not hurt me: forasmuch as before him innocency was found in me**; and also before thee, O king, have I done no hurt."*

   D.   Moses

        1.   Hebrews 11:24-27 - *"²⁴By faith Moses, when he was come to years, refused to be called the son of Pharaoh's daughter; ²⁵**Choosing rather to suffer affliction** with the people of God, than to enjoy the pleasures of sin for a season; ²⁶**Esteeming the reproach of Christ** greater riches than the treasures in Egypt: for he had respect unto the recompence of the reward.*

> *²⁷By **faith he forsook Egypt, not fearing the wrath of the king: for he endured, as seeing him who is invisible**.*"

E.   Shadrach, Meshach, and Abednego

  1.   Daniel 3:15-18 - "*¹⁵Now if ye be ready that at what time ye hear the sound of the cornet, flute, harp, sackbut, psaltery, and dulcimer, and all kinds of musick, ye fall down and **worship the image which I have made**; well: but if ye worship not, ye shall be cast* the same hour *into the midst of a burning fiery furnace; and who is that God that shall deliver you out of my hands?* ¹⁶**Shadrach, Meshach, and Abednego, answered** *and said to the king, O Nebuchadnezzar, we are not careful to answer thee in this matter.* ¹⁷**If it be so, our God whom we serve is able to deliver us from the burning fiery furnace, and he will deliver us out of thine hand, O king.** ¹⁸**But if not, be it known unto thee, O king, that we will not serve thy gods, nor worship the golden image which thou hast set up.**"

These are great examples of men of God who put their trust in God and nothing could make them afraid. They loved not their life unto the end. The last day's sons of God will be like them (Revelation 12:11). Nothing and nobody will make them afraid. And look at their end and what it brought to others also:

Daniel 3:23-25, 27-29 - "²³And **these three men**, Shadrach, Meshach, and Abednego, **fell down <u>bound</u> into** the midst of **the burning fiery furnace**. ²⁴Then Nebuchadnezzar the king was astonied, and rose up in haste, and spake, and said unto his counsellors, Did not we cast three men bound into the midst of the fire? They answered and said unto the king, True, O king. ²⁵He answered and said, Lo, **I see four men loose, walking in the midst of the fire, and they have no hurt**; and the form of the fourth is like the Son of God.. 27And the princes, governors, and captains, and the king's counsellors, being gathered together, saw **these men, upon whose bodies the fire had no power, nor was an hair of their head singed, neither were their coats changed, nor the smell of fire had passed on them**. 28 [Then] Nebuchadnezzar spake, and said, Blessed [be] the God of Shadrach, Meshach, and Abed-nego, who hath sent his angel, and delivered his servants that trusted in him, and have changed the king's word, and yielded their bodies, that they might not serve nor worship any god, except their own God. **29 Therefore I make a decree, That every people, nation, and language,** *which speak any thing amiss against the God of Shadrach, Meshach, and Abed-nego, shall be cut in pieces, and their houses shall be made a dunghill: because there is no other God that can deliver after this sort."*

This is what will happen when you trust in God rather than fear death. When we step out in faith and trust in God, we will be free from fear and all things that bound us. We can see the salvation of the Lord, and not just us but all the people around us. When people see what God has done in our lives, they will fear God. God will allow us to go through great trials, but He always has something greater in mind. Many times people just need to witness God's deliverance in our lives and that will make them want to serve our God. Praise be to Jesus! Personally, when I saw what Jesus had done for me; what He suffered so I wouldn't have to, it just breaks my heart and makes me want to serve Him.

F. Paul

1. Acts 18:9-11 - *"⁹Then **spake the Lord to Paul** in the night by a vision, **Be not afraid, but speak, and hold not thy peace**: ¹⁰**For I am with thee, and no man shall set on thee to hurt thee**: for I have much people in this city. ¹¹**And he continued** there a year and six months, teaching the **word of God** among them."*

2. 2 Corinthians 1:7-11 - *"⁷And our hope of you is stedfast, knowing, that as ye are partakers of the sufferings, so shall ye be also of the consolation. ⁸For we would not, **brethren, have you ignorant of our trouble which came to us in Asia**, that we were pressed out of measure, above strength, insomuch that we despaired even of life: ⁹But **we had the sentence of death in ourselves**, that we should not trust in ourselves, but in **God which raiseth the dead**: ¹⁰**Who delivered us from so great a death**, and **doth deliver**: in whom we trust that **he will yet deliver us**; ¹¹Ye also helping together by prayer for us, that for the gift bestowed upon us by the means of many persons thanks may be given by many on our behalf."*

3. 2 Corinthians 4:8-12 - *"⁸**We are troubled on every side**, yet not distressed; we are perplexed, but not in despair; ⁹Persecuted, but not forsaken; cast down, but not destroyed; ¹⁰**Always bearing about in the body the dying of the Lord Jesus**, that the life also of Jesus might be made manifest in our body. ¹¹**For we which live are alway delivered unto death for Jesus' sake**, that the life also of Jesus might be made*

        manifest in our mortal flesh. ^{12} So then **death worketh in us, but life in you**."
    4. 1 Corinthians 4:9 - "*For I think that God hath set forth* **us the apostles last, as it were appointed to death**: *for we are made a spectacle unto the world, and to angels, and to men.*"
    5. 2 Corinthians 11:23 - "***Are they ministers of Christ?*** *(I speak as a fool) I am more; in labours more abundant, in stripes above measure, in prisons more frequent,* **in deaths oft**."

Paul also said that apostles were appointed to death. That speaks to all of us who wants to be His faithful disciples, we are also appointed to death. Not necessarily a natural death but a dying to our fleshly, carnal nature. Psalms 116:15 says "*Precious in the sight of the Lord [is] the death of his saints.*" Paul also said "I die daily" (1 Corinthians 15:31). In Luke 9:23 Jesus says "*If any [man] will come after me, let him deny himself, and take up his cross daily, and follow me.*" Cross in the Greek means cross (as an instrument of capital punishment), tool of execution. Jesus asked His disciples that daily pick up the tool of their execution. This doesn't mean they physically died daily, but that they died to the "deeds of their body" (Romans 8:13). They died to those carnal, worldly things that stood between them and the Kingdom of God. Jesus desire is that we would die to all those things and live for heavenly things. This doesn't mean we can't enjoy life, because Jesus came so we might have life and have it more abundantly (John 10:10). The important thing is that Jesus would sit on the throne of our hearts and that He is the first in our lives and obey his voice.

V. God's Promise to His Bride

There are so many more examples of those that preached the Kingdom of God in spite of persecution, but I just picked a couple. This is what is said about the Overcomers: Revelation 12:11 - "*And they overcame him by the blood of the Lamb, and by the word of their testimony; and* **they loved not their lives unto the death**." To all those whom willing to risk their lives, God promises great rewards.

    A. Matthew 16:28 - "*Verily I say unto you,* **There be some standing here, which shall not taste of death, till they see the Son of man coming in his kingdom**."

        1. Mark 9:1 - "*And he said unto them, Verily I say unto you, That there be some of them that stand here, which shall not taste of*

        death, till they have seen the kingdom of God come with power."
- 2. Luke 9:27 - ***"But I tell you of a truth, there be some standing here, which shall not taste of death, till they see the kingdom of God."***
- B. John 8:51 - *"Verily, verily, I say unto you, **<u>If a man keep my saying, he shall never see death</u>**."*
- C. 1 Corinthians 15:51,53 - *"Behold, I shew you a mystery; **We shall not all sleep, but we shall all be changed.** 53 For this corruptible must put on incorruption, and this mortal [must] put on immortality."* – In another words, not everybody will die but everybody will be changed.

- D. Hebrews 11:5 - *"**<u>By faith Enoch was translated that he should not see death</u>**; and was not found, because God had translated him: for before his translation he had this testimony, that he pleased God."*

    Enoch walked with God and was not. What a great testimony! He didn't have to experience death, God simply took him. (Genesis 5:24 - *"And Enoch walked with God: and he [was] not; for God took him."*

- E. Esther 4:7-8, 10-16 - *"⁷And Mordecai told him of all that had happened unto him, and of the sum of the money that Haman had promised to pay to the king's treasuries for the Jews, to destroy them. ⁸Also he gave him the copy of the writing of the decree that was given at Shushan to destroy them, **to shew it unto Esther, and to declare it unto her, and to charge her that she should go in unto the king, to make supplication unto him, and to make request before him for her people**... ¹⁰Again **Esther spake** unto Hatach, and gave him commandment unto Mordecai; ¹¹ All the king's servants, and the people of the king's provinces, do know, that **whosoever**, whether man or woman, **shall come unto the king into the inner court, who is not called, there is one law of his to put him to death,** except such to whom the king shall hold out the golden sceptre, that he may live: but I have not been called to come in unto the king these thirty days... ¹³Then Mordecai commanded to answer Esther, **Think not with thyself that thou shalt escape in the king's house,** more than all the Jews. ¹⁴**For if thou altogether holdest thy peace** at this time, then shall there enlargement and **deliverance arise to the Jews from another place**; but thou and thy father's house shall be destroyed: and who* *knoweth whether thou art come to the kingdom for such a time as this?* ¹⁵Then **Esther bade them return Mordecai this answer**, ¹⁶*Go, gather together all the Jews that are present in Shushan, and fast ye for me, and neither eat nor drink three days, night or day: I also and my maidens will fast likewise; and* **so will I go in unto the king, which is not according to the law: and if I perish, I perish**.*"*

Esther feared for her life and Mordecai told her if she wouldn't go, God would appoint another and she will be lost. So she went before the king in spite of fear of her own life and on the behalf of her people. By doing that, she saved a whole nation. What a great example of she is. Our decisions effect others also, that's why it's important us to obey God's words and don't let the enemy stop us in that.

 F. Judges 6:23 – *"And the LORD said unto him (Gideon),* **Peace be unto thee; fear not:** *thou shalt not die."*

Gideon was also afraid of death, but it didn't stop him from fulfilling the calling of God on His life. We should not fear death *"For the law of the Spirit of life in Christ Jesus hath made me free from the law of sin and death."* and because *"to be carnally minded is death; but to be spiritually minded is life and peace."* (Romans 8:2, 6).

God's promise is that He will *"deliver them who through fear of death were all their lifetime subject to bondage."* (Hebrews 2:15) and that *"The* **last enemy that shall be destroyed is death***...So when this corruptible shall have put on incorruption, and this mortal shall have put on immortality, then shall be brought to pass the saying that is written,* **Death is swallowed up in victory.** ⁵⁵**O death, where is thy sting? O grave, where is thy victory**? ⁵⁶*The sting of death is sin; and the strength of sin is the law.* ⁵⁷**But thanks be to God, which giveth us the victory through our Lord Jesus Christ.** ⁵⁸**<u>Therefore</u>, my beloved brethren, be ye stedfast, unmoveable, always abounding in the work of the Lord, forasmuch as ye know that your labour is not in vain in the Lord.***"* (1 Corinthians 15:26, 54-58) and also that at the end *"***God shall wipe away all tears from their eyes; and there shall be no more death, neither sorrow, nor crying, neither shall there be any more pain: for the former things are passed away.***"* (Revelation 21:4) Hallelujah! Glory to God Almighty! Glory to Jesus!

Chapter VI

Fear of Inadequacy

In Job 32:6 Elihu said to the other comforters *"**I am young**, and ye are very old; wherefore **I was afraid**, and durst not shew you mine opinion."* Elihu had waited until Job and his three friends stopped talking. He was afraid to speak because he felt inadequate, because all of them were older than him. As we search the Scriptures, we found that others were dealing with insecurities because of their age or inexperience. We need to remember though that *"Great men are not always wise: neither do the aged understand judgment."* (Job 32:9) Let us consider how men of God overcame their fear of inadequacy.

I. Timothy

This is what Paul said to Timothy who was pretty young when Paul sent him out to minister.

- A. 1 Timothy 4:12 - *"**Let no man despise thy youth**; but be thou an example of the believers, in word, in conversation, in charity, in spirit, in faith, in purity."*
- B. 2 Timothy 1:7 - *"For **God hath not given us the spirit of fear**; but of power, and of love, and of a sound mind."*

This word fear in the Greek means timidity. We shouldn't be timid, but we need to stir up the gift of God within ourselves because we have the Spirit of God, of power, and of love in us.

II. Joshua

Joshua was afraid when Moses put him to charge to take the Israelites into the Promise land, but Moses, and then God said this to him:

- A. Deuteronomy 31:7-8 - *"⁷And Moses called unto Joshua, and said unto him in the sight of all Israel, **Be strong and of a good courage:** for thou must go with this people unto the land which the LORD hath sworn unto their fathers to give them; and thou shalt cause them to inherit it. ⁸And the LORD, he it is that doth go before* *thee; he will be with thee, he will not fail thee, neither forsake thee: **fear not, neither be dismayed.**"*

God told Joshua three times don't be afraid and to be strong and of a good courage because He will not forsake him, and as He was with Moses so He would be with Joshua also.

    B. Joshua 1:9 - *"**Have not I commanded thee**? Be strong and of a good courage; **be not afraid, neither be thou dismayed**: for the LORD thy God is with thee whithersoever thou goest."*

After this the people themselves were encouraging Joshua and promised him that they will obey him.

    C. Joshua 1:17-18 - *"¹⁷According as we hearkened unto Moses in all things, so will we hearken unto thee: only the LORD thy God be with thee, as he was with Moses. ¹⁸**Whosoever he be that doth rebel against thy commandment, and will not hearken unto thy words in all that thou commandest him, he shall be put to death: <u>only be strong and of a good courage</u>.*"

We should be confident and shouldn't fear and shouldn't feel inadequate if God is with us. We are only vessels anyway. It's not us, but God within us that matters. *"God delights not in a leg of a man."* (Psalms 147:10). Zechariah 4:6 says *"Not by might, nor by power, but by my Spirit sayeth the Lord."*. If we obey God we don't need to fear because we won't act out of our own strength but through God's Spirit and power.

III. Solomon

Solomon was young and tender as David said it in 1 Chronicles 29:1: "Furthermore David the king said unto all the congregation, **Solomon my son**, whom alone God hath chosen, is **yet young and tender**..." The word "tender" also means weak. But David, being a good father, prepared for him everything that he would need to complete the call that he was called to. He also didn't leave him alone; besides God, he had helpers, willing men, priests, etc along the way. So Solomon had no reason to fear. **If God appoints you to do something, it doesn't matter how young, weak, or inexperienced you are, you don't need to fear, He will take care of you**. Just do whatever He commands you to do. Obey His voice.

A. 1 Chronicles 28:20-21 - *"²⁰And David said to Solomon his son, **Be strong and of good courage, and do it: fear not, nor be dismayed**: for the LORD God, even my God, will be with thee; he will not fail thee, nor forsake thee, until thou hast finished all the work for the service of the house of the LORD. ²¹And, behold, the courses of the priests and the Levites, even they shall be with thee for all the service of the house of God: and there shall be with thee for all manner of workmanship every willing skilful man, for any manner of service: also the princes and all the people will be wholly at thy commandment."*

B. 1 Chronicles 22:5 - *"And David said, **Solomon my son is young and tender**, and the house that is to be builded for the LORD must be exceeding magnifical, of fame and of glory throughout all countries: I will **therefore now make preparation for it, so David prepared abundantly before his death**."*

David is a wonderful example of a great, godly father. So if you belong to a local church that God appointed you to and you have the father in the Lord that God appointed for you, you don't need to fear because he prepared everything for you to carry on the calling of that ministry, the calling of God. You just need to be obedient and you don't need to feel inadequate and weak!

God encouraged Jacob with the same encouragement that He encouraged Joshua, and David said the same to Solomon. (Genesis 28:15 - *"And, behold, I am with thee, and will keep thee in all places whither thou goest, and will bring thee again into this land; for I will not leave thee, until I have done that which I have spoken to thee of."*) They encouraged each other with the same encouragement with which they were encouraged.

IV. Gideon

A. Judges 6:14-17 - *"¹⁶And the LORD looked upon him, and said, **Go in this thy might, and thou shalt save Israel from the***

hand of the Midianites: have not I sent thee? ^{15} ***And he said unto him, Oh my Lord, wherewith shall I save Israel? behold, my family is poor in Manasseh, and I am the least in my father's house.*** ^{16}*And the LORD said unto him, Surely I will be with thee, and thou shalt smite the Midianites as one man.* ^{17}*And he said unto him, If now I have found grace in thy sight, then shew me a sign that thou talkest with me."*

Gideon was first afraid when God was telling him that He would deliver Israel through Gideon and only Gideon's hands. He was scared that he didn't hear God, so he tested Him three times. Then, once he recognized God's messenger, he was afraid because he saw him face to face and because he doubted God. He wasn't sure that he could do what God asked him to do. But God proved Himself faithful to him over and over again. God knows that we are nothing, but through Him we can move mountains. He will never leave us alone if he commanded something from us and He never asks anything from us that we could not do without His help, therefore we have no reason to fear. He is always present to help us, so we just need to obey His words.

V. Moses

A. Exodus 3:4-22 - "^{4}*And when the LORD saw that he turned aside to see,* **God called unto him out of the midst of the bush**, *and said, Moses, Moses. And* **he said, Here am I**... ^{6}*Moreover he said, I am the God of thy father, the God of Abraham, the God of Isaac, and the God of Jacob. And* **Moses hid his face; for he was afraid to look upon God**. ^{7}***And the LORD said****, I have surely seen the affliction of my people which are in Egypt, and have heard their cry by reason of their taskmasters; for I know their sorrows;*

*⁸And **I am come down to deliver them** out of the hand of the Egyptians, and to bring them up out of that land unto a good land and a large, unto a land flowing with milk and honey; unto the place of the Canaanites, and the Hittites, and the Amorites, and the Perizzites, and the Hivites, and the Jebusites... ¹⁰**Come now therefore, and I will send thee** unto Pharaoh, that **thou mayest bring forth my people** the children of Israel out of Egypt. ¹¹And Moses said unto God, Who am I, that I should go unto Pharaoh, and that I should bring forth the children of Israel out of Egypt? ¹²And **he said, Certainly I will be with thee; and this shall be a token unto thee, that I have sent thee:** When thou hast brought forth the people out of Egypt, ye shall serve God upon this mountain. ¹³And Moses said unto God, Behold, when I come unto the children of Israel, and shall say unto them, The God of your fathers hath sent me unto you; and they shall say to me, What is his name? what shall I say unto them?** ¹⁴And God said unto Moses, I AM THAT I AM: and he said, Thus shalt thou say unto the children of Israel, I AM hath sent me unto you... And I have said, I will bring you up out of the affliction of Egypt unto the land of the Canaanites, and the Hittites, and the Amorites, and the Perizzites, and the Hivites, and the Jebusites, unto a land flowing with milk and honey. ¹⁸**And they shall hearken to thy voice:** and thou shalt come, thou and the elders of Israel, unto the king of Egypt, and ye shall say unto him, The LORD God of the Hebrews hath met with us: and now let us go, we beseech thee, three days' journey into the wilderness, that we may sacrifice to the LORD our God. ¹⁹**And I am sure that the king of Egypt will not let you go,** no, not by a mighty hand. ²⁰**And I will stretch out my hand, and smite Egypt** with all my wonders which I will do in the midst thereof: and after that he will let you go..."*

> B. Exodus 4:1-16 - *"¹And **Moses answered and said, But, behold, they will not believe me, nor hearken unto my voice: for they will say, The LORD hath not appeared unto thee.** ²And the **LORD said unto him, What is that in thine hand?** And he said, A rod. ³And he said, Cast it on the ground. And he cast it on the ground, and it became a serpent; and Moses fled from before it. ⁴And the LORD said unto Moses, Put forth thine hand, and take it by the tail. And he put forth his hand, and caught it, and it became a rod in his hand: ⁵**That they may believe that the LORD God of their fathers, the God of Abraham, the God of Isaac, and the God of Jacob, hath appeared unto thee...** And it shall come to pass, **if they will not believe thee, neither hearken to the voice of the first sign, that they will believe the voice of the latter sign.** ⁹And** it shall come to pass, if they **will not believe also these two signs, neither hearken unto thy voice, that thou shalt take of the water of the river, and pour***

*it upon the dry land: and the water which thou takest out of **the river shall become blood** upon the dry land.* ¹⁰***And Moses said unto the LORD, O my Lord, I am not eloquent, neither heretofore, nor since thou hast spoken unto thy servant: but I am slow of speech, and of a slow tongue.*** ¹¹***And the LORD said unto him, Who hath made man's mouth? or who maketh the dumb, or deaf, or the seeing, or the blind? have not I the LORD?*** ¹²*Now therefore go, and I will be with thy mouth, and teach thee what thou shalt say.* ¹³ ***And he said, O my Lord, send, I pray thee, by the hand of him whom thou wilt send.*** ¹⁴***And the anger of the LORD was kindled against Moses***, *and he said, Is not Aaron the Levite thy brother? I know that he can speak well. And also, behold, he cometh forth to meet thee: and when he seeth thee, he will be glad in his heart.* ¹⁵*And thou shalt speak unto him, and put words in his mouth: and I will be with thy mouth, and with his mouth, and will teach you what ye shall do.* ¹⁶***And he shall be thy spokesman unto the people: and he shall be, even he shall be to thee instead of a mouth, and thou shalt be to him instead of God.***"

Moses, in front of the burning bush, was afraid his speech would be inadequate. It is crazy how many excuses Moses gave God. I encourage you to read these two chapters. The only thing that Moses did without questioning was to turn and hearken to God's voice when He spoke out of the bush. But from there on, it didn't matter what God said to him, he was fearful. He was afraid that nobody would believe him; no one would do what God had instructed, etc. We have a merciful God who is so patient. He put up Moses' insecurities for a long time because He is a merciful God and *"searcheth the heart and the inward parts of man"*. But even God himself got angry with Moses towards the end. Moses definitely wasn't the great example of faith then. Still, God didn't forsake him, because He saw something in him that I bet Moses didn't even know about himself. God knows the end from the beginning. Hallelujah!

VI. <u>Isaiah</u>

    A. Isaiah 6:5 - *"Then said I, Woe is me! for I am undone; because I am a man of unclean lips, and I dwell in the midst of a people of unclean lips: for mine eyes have seen the King, the LORD of hosts."*

Isaiah saw his own down falls. He was too unclean to speak, he saw his iniquities, weaknesses, but God has a provision for that. He doesn't leave us like that. In this case, He sent cherubims with a coal from the altar and purged Isaiah's sins.

VII. Saul

    A. 1 Samuel 9:20-21 *"²⁰And as for thine asses that were lost three days ago, set not thy mind on them; for they are found. And on whom is all the desire of Israel? Is it not on thee, and on all thy father's house? ²¹* **And Saul answered and said, Am not I a Benjamite, of the smallest of the tribes of Israel? and my family the least of all the families of the tribe of Benjamin? wherefore then speakest thou so to me?"**

    B. 1 Samuel 10:21-23 - *"²¹When he had caused the tribe of Benjamin to come near by their families, the family of Matri was taken, and Saul the son of Kish was taken: and* **when they sought him, he could not be found.** *²²Therefore they enquired of the LORD further, if the man should yet come thither. And the LORD answered, Behold,* **he hath hid himself among the stuff.** *²³And they ran and fetched him thence: and when he stood among the people, he was higher than any of the people from his shoulders and upward."* - Saul hid when he was first called to be king, because he didn't think much of himself.

David was a great example of those that didn't even give a little place to the fear of inadequacy. First of all when Samuel went to David's father house to anoint the next king, David's father didn't even think to bring David before Samuel until Samuel was keep asking about him (1 Samuel 16:11 – *"And Samuel said unto Jesse, Are here all thy children? And he said, There remaineth yet the youngest, and, behold, he keepeth the sheep. And Samuel said unto Jesse, Send and fetch him: for we will not sit down till he come hither"*) Then later on Saul and David's brothers all thought that David was inadequate when he about to face Goliath. They called him prideful (1 Samuel 17:28-42). But David didn't care; he didn't allow anyone to define him other than God. Saul called him young and inexperienced (verse 33). Then Goliath disdained him because of his youth (verse 42). But no one could stop him. He wasn't going to allow anyone to defy the armies of the living God. He knew Jesus, had an intimate knowledge of the Lord of Hosts, and he knew that it was not himself that would bring the victory anyways, but the Almighty God. David knew that salvation is of the Lord and he was just a willing vessel (verse 47).

Jesus also encourages us with this: Luke 21:14-15 says *"¹⁴****Settle it therefore in your hearts, not to meditate before what ye shall answer:***

*15For **I will give you a mouth and wisdom, which all your adversaries shall not be able to gainsay nor resist**."*

Let me finish with this. Even if we try our best we will fall occasionally until we reach perfection, so why are we losing sleep over it? Isaiah 40:30: *"Even the youths shall faint and be weary, and **the young men shall utterly fall**:"* **Until we reach full maturity in God, completeness, we will make mistakes, we will fall. But being afraid because of it could stop us walking in obedience to God.** So we need to cast down all of those fears and only listen what God says.

Chapter VII

Being Afraid of God

Jacob said called the house of God a dreadful place (Genesis 28:17). Wherever God is present can be a fearful place because of His power and majesty. The Scriptures command us to fear God, and we ought to do it, but He doesn't want us to be afraid of Him. We need to respect and honor Him, but we shouldn't flee from His presence.

I. Examples of the fear of God of God's people

    A. Exodus 19:16 – *"And it came to pass on the third day in the morning, that there were thunders and lightnings, and a thick cloud upon the mount, and the voice of the trumpet exceeding loud; so that **all the people that was in the camp trembled**."*

Israel was greatly afraid of God and it stopped them from going into His presence and because of that they missed out on a deep intimate fellowship with God.

    B. Exodus 20:19-20 – *"And they said unto Moses, Speak thou with us, and we will hear: but **let not God speak with us, lest we die**. And Moses said unto the people, **Fear not**: for God is come to prove you, and that his fear may be before your faces, that ye sin not."*

A healthy fear and reverence of God causes us to not sin anymore, but simply being afraid of him causes us to run from Him, like Adam and Eve did.

    C. Genesis 28:17 – *"And **he was afraid, and said, How dreadful is this place**! this is none other but the house of God, and this is the gate of heaven."*

Jacob was afraid, but that didn't stop him from having a relationship with God. Wherever God is, it is dreadful because He is the Almighty, all powerful God. But He is also gentle, loving and merciful. We should not to be afraid of Him.

    D. Job 23:15 – *"Therefore am **I troubled at his presence: when I consider, I am afraid of him**."*

Many times when God's dealing with us we become fearful. We are afraid of what He might allows in our lives, what He will do to us. In that case we just need to remind ourselves of His mercy and grace and love, and that everything He allows in our lives will work together for good in the end. If we do this, fear will flee. Just like when the devil tried to temp Jesus in the wilderness. Jesus resisted him, and he left Him for a season (Luke 4:13). Same things happen with fear also.

> E. Mark 9:6 - *"For he wist not what to say; **for they were sore afraid**."* (Luke 9:34 - *"While he thus spake, there came a cloud, and overshadowed them: and **they feared as they entered into the cloud**."*)

This happened at the mount of transfiguration. Peter, James, and John went up the mountain with Jesus. But when Jesus transfigured before them, they were extremely afraid. The presence of God is a "dreadful" place, but it is also the most beautiful, peaceful, restful place. **Once we see God that closely, it could be frightening because He is the Perfection of Beauty. When we stand in His presence we can see how short we fall and how far we are from that Beauty. But we need to be encouraged because we are on the road**, we have already left and we are much better off than we were before. If we continue follow God's path for us, there shall be a day when we can see Him as He is and out of us He will shine.

Psalms 119:120 says, *"My flesh trembleth for fear of thee; and I am afraid of thy judgments."* **Even David was afraid of God and His judgment, still it didn't stop Him from drawing closer. It just made him respect God even more.** This is the difference between these three (Moses, David, and Job) and Israel in the wilderness: when the Glory of God was present, Israel got scared and denied to enter in, but these three men entered in despite their fear. Don't let fear keep you away from the presence of God. God wants us to run to Him. He is our refuge, He is our strength. Don't be afraid of Him!

> F. Acts 10:4 - *"And **when he looked on him, he was afraid**, and said, What is it, Lord? And he said unto him, Thy prayers and thine alms are come up for a memorial before God."*

Cornelius was afraid, nevertheless he moved on the Word of God and didn't hide or run in fear. Like I said before, God doesn't want us to be afraid of Him, but we should fear Him, honor Him, and that makes us wants to do the will of God. ("Hebrews 11:7 *"By faith Noah, being warned of God of things not seen as yet, moved **with fear, prepared an ark** to the saving of his house; by the which he condemned the world, and became heir of the righteousness which is by faith."*)

    G.   Luke 2:8-9 - *"⁸And there were in the same country **shepherds abiding in the field**, keeping watch over their flock by night. ⁹And, lo, the angel of the Lord came upon them, and **the glory of the Lord shone round about them: and they were sore afraid**."*

    H.   The woman with the issue of blood

        1.   Mark 5:33 - *"But the **woman fearing and trembling**, knowing what was done in her, **came and fell down before him**, and told him all the truth."*

        2.   Luke 8:47 - *"And when the woman saw that she was not hid, she came trembling, and falling down before him, **she declared unto him before all the people** for what cause she had touched him, and how she was healed immediately."*

Her fear didn't stop her from going to Jesus and honoring Him and declaring before all people what Jesus had done in her life.

    I.   Acts 9:6 - *"And **he trembling and astonished** said, Lord, what wilt thou have me to do? And the Lord said unto him, Arise, and go into the city, and it shall be told thee what thou must do."*

This happened to Saul. But again, he obeyed God's word despite his fears.

II.   Nevertheless God uses fear to restore respect to Him and to His people

Many times we don't listen God's gentle warnings and in that case He uses fear to make us go back to Him, but this is not His first choice.

    A.   Acts 5:11 – *"And **great fear came upon all the church**, and upon as many as heard these things."*

    B.   1 Samuel 11:7 – *"And he took a yoke of oxen, and hewed them in pieces, and sent them throughout all the coasts of Israel by the hands of messengers, saying, Whosoever cometh not forth after Saul* *and after Samuel, so shall it be done unto his oxen. And the **fear of the LORD fell on the people**, and they came out with one consent."*

See the difference in Saul's and the people's heart between 1 Samuel 11:7 and chapter 17:11. 1 Samuel 17:11 says *"When Saul and all Israel heard those words of the Philistine, they were dismayed, and greatly afraid."* What a difference! When we fear and trust God our whole heart, nothing can makes us afraid. As soon as the fear of God departs from us anything can scares us. Our fear of God makes nations and the people around us to respect us, but if we don't fear God and don't trust Him and we're full of fear this will weaken and discourage those people around us also.

When we fear God, it causes the unity of the saints and the respect of the nations around us. But when we don't trust Him and are afraid, confusion and a feebleness of the heart will be our end.

C. Esther 8:17 – *"And **many of the people of the land became Jews; for the fear of the Jews** fell upon them."*
D. Acts 5:11, 14 – *"And **great fear** came upon all the church, and upon as many as heard these things. **And believers were the more added to the Lord**, multitudes both of men and women."*
E. Isaiah 66:4 - *"I also will choose their delusions, and **will bring their fears upon them**; because when I called, none did answer; when I spake, they did not hear: but they did evil before mine eyes, and chose that in which I delighted not."*

Sometimes the only thing can bring us back to God that He allows things of our lives that makes us frightened. God uses everything just so He wouldn't lose us, even that we may consider "bad" things He allows it in our lives for our sake. First though He tries to gently warn us, but if we don't listen to Him He uses more "heavy weaponry".

F. Jeremiah 20:4 - *"For thus saith the LORD, Behold, **I will make thee a terror to thyself**, and to all thy friends: and they shall fall by the sword of their enemies, and thine eyes shall behold it: and I will give all Judah into the hand of the king of Babylon, and he shall carry them captive into Babylon, and shall slay them with the sword."* - **God uses fear to draw more people to Himself, but that's not His first choice.**
G. Luke 1:63-66 *"⁶³And he asked for a writing table, and wrote, saying, His name is John. And they marvelled all. ⁶⁴And **his mouth was opened immediately**, and his tongue loosed, and he spake, and praised God. ⁶⁵And **fear came on all that dwelt round about***

***them**: and all these sayings were noised abroad throughout all the hill country of Judaea. ⁶⁶And all they that heard them laid them up in their hearts, saying, What manner of child shall this be! And the hand of the Lord was with him."*

H. Acts 2:43 - ***"And fear came upon every soul: and many wonders and signs were done by the apostles."*** - When God does a great miracle, it makes people respect Him and fear Him.

III. The Gentiles will fear God

Isn't it interesting that the heathens fear God because they recognize His mighty, powerful nature, but Pharisees would rather fear men than God. See how religion blinds you.

A. John 19:7-8 - *"⁷The Jews answered him, We have a law, and by our law he ought to die, because he made himself the Son of God. ⁸When **Pilate** therefore heard that saying, **he was the more afraid**;"*

B. Matthew 27:54 - *"Now **when the centurion**, and they that were with him, **watching Jesus**, saw the earthquake, **and those things that were done, they feared greatly**, saying, **Truly this was the Son of God.**"*

C. Mark 5:13-15 - *"¹³And forthwith Jesus gave them leave. **And the unclean spirits went out**, and entered into the swine: and the herd ran violently down a steep place into the sea, (they were about two thousand;) and were choked in the sea. ¹⁴**And they that fed the swine fled, and told it in the city**, and in the country. And they went out to see what it was that was done. ¹⁵**And they come to Jesus**, and see him that was possessed with the devil, and had the legion, sitting, and clothed, and in his right mind: **and they were afraid.**"*

D. Matthew 21:10 - *"And when he was come into Jerusalem, **all the city was moved**, saying, Who is this?"*

E. Matthew 27:51 - *"And, behold, the veil of the temple was rent in twain from the top to the bottom; and the **earth did quake**, and the rocks rent;"*

F. 1 Samuel 4:5-8 - *"⁵And **when the ark of the covenant of the LORD** came into the camp, all Israel shouted with a great shout, so that the earth rang again. ⁶**And when the Philistines heard the noise of the shout**, they said, What meaneth the noise of this great shout in the camp of the Hebrews? And **they understood that the ark of the LORD was come into the camp**. ⁷And the Philistines were* *afraid, for they said, God is come into the camp. And they said, Woe unto us! for there hath not been such a thing heretofore. ⁸**Woe unto us! who shall deliver us out of the hand of these mighty Gods?** these are the Gods that smote the Egyptians with all the plagues in the wilderness."*

VI. The devil is afraid of God

    A. James 2:19 - *"Thou believest that there is one God; thou doest well: **the devils also believe, and tremble**."*

Chapter VIII

Fear of God's Judgment

There are times when God allows hard things to happen to us. When we don't obey His voice or when we become really rebellious, that's the only way He can make us turn back to Him. But even then, we don't need to fear because as soon as we truly repent and forsake our evil ways, He will have mercy upon us and He will restore us. For example: the prodigal son in Luke 15. He wasted his possession, and he left his father's house. But the father was waiting for him the whole time and when he finally came back, the father gave him a ring, robe etc. Our misery only lasts until we bow our knees and let His will be done and not ours. Once we've done that, God will come skipping and running with joy to our aid.

I. Few examples for when God allows horrible things in his people's lives just to bring them back to Himself

    A. Leviticus 26:14, 16 - "But **if ye will not hearken unto me**, and will not do all these commandments; I also will do this unto you; **I will even appoint over you terror**, consumption, and the burning ague, that shall consume the eyes, and cause sorrow of heart: and ye shall sow your seed in vain, for your enemies shall eat it." Then He finishes it like this in verse 44, 45: "And **yet for all that**, when they be in the land of their enemies, **I will not cast them away**, neither will I abhor them, to destroy them utterly, **and to break my covenant** with them: **for I am the LORD their God. But I will for their sakes remember the covenant of their ancestors**, whom I brought forth out of the land of Egypt in the sight of the heathen, that I might be their God: I am the LORD."
    B. Jeremiah 8:14, 15 - " Why do we sit still? assemble yourselves, and let us enter into the defenced cities, and let us be silent there: for the LORD our God hath put us to silence, and given us water of gall to drink, because we have sinned against the LORD. We looked for peace, but no good came; and for a time of health, and behold trouble!"
    C. Jeremiah 19:3-4 - "And say, Hear ye the word of the LORD, O kings of Judah, and inhabitants of Jerusalem; Thus saith the LORD of hosts, the God of Israel; Behold, **I will bring evil upon this place**, the **which whosoever heareth, his ears shall tingle**. 4 Because they have forsaken me, and have estranged this place, and have

burned incense in it unto other gods, whom neither they nor their fathers have known, nor the kings of Judah, and have filled this place with the blood of innocents;"

The meaning of the word "Tingle" is, the idea of *vibration*); to *tinkle*, that is, *rattle* together (as the ears in *reddening* with shame, or the teeth in *chattering* with fear **We fear because we have sinned against God. In this case we have to repent and turn to God again.**

- D. Jude 1:23 - *"And others save with fear, pulling them out of the fire; hating even the garment spotted by the flesh."*

II. God is faithful even if we have messed up

Sometimes when we mess up terribly, we are afraid of God's judgment upon us, but let me tell you, God doesn't want us to be afraid. He wants us to repent and turn back to Him and His ways. **God has a provision for us, even if we have messed up terribly. We don't have to fear if we mess up because if we repent, He'll heal us and restore us. Nothing can separate us from the love of God!**

- A. Jeremiah 30:5, 7, 10-24 (Jer. 46:27-28) – *"For thus saith the LORD; We have heard a **voice of trembling, of fear, and not of peace**... Alas! for that day is great, so that none is like it: it is even the time of Jacob's trouble; <u>but</u> he shall <u>be saved out of it</u>... **Therefore fear thou not**, O my servant Jacob, saith the LORD; neither be dismayed, O Israel: **for, lo, I will save thee from afar**, and thy seed from the land of their captivity; and Jacob shall return, and shall be in rest, and be quiet, and **none shall make him afraid**. For I am with thee, saith the LORD, to save thee: though I make a full end of all nations whither I have scattered thee, yet will I not make a full end of thee: **but I will correct thee in measure, and will not leave thee altogether unpunished**... All thy lovers have forgotten thee; they seek thee not; for **I have wounded thee with the wound of an enemy**, with the chastisement of a cruel one, for the multitude of thine iniquity; because thy sins were increased... <u>**For I will restore health unto thee, and I will heal thee of thy wounds, saith the LORD**</u>; because they called thee an Outcast, saying, This is Zion, whom no man seeketh after."* - He is a faithful, loving God!

B. Judges 6:10 – *"And I said unto you, I am the LORD your God; **fear not** the gods of the Amorites, in whose land ye dwell: but ye have not obeyed my voice."*

Even if we don't obey His voice, He sends us a messenger to help us and deliver us through. He sent Gideon. He doesn't give up on us that easily. Thank you Jesus for your mercy!

C. 1 Samuel 12:12,14-25 - *"And when ye saw that Nahash the king of the children of Ammon came against you, ye said unto me, Nay; but a king shall reign over us: when the LORD your God was your king... If ye will fear the LORD, and serve him, and obey his voice, and not rebel against the commandment of the LORD, then shall both ye and also the king that reigneth over you continue following the LORD your God: But **if ye will not obey the voice of the LORD, but rebel against** the commandment of the LORD, **then shall the hand of the LORD be against you**, as it was against your fathers... Is it not wheat harvest to day? I will call unto the LORD, and he shall send thunder and rain; that ye may perceive and see that your wickedness is great, which ye have done in the sight of the LORD, in asking you a king. So Samuel called unto the LORD; and the **LORD sent thunder and rain that day: and all the people greatly feared the LORD and Samuel. And all the people said unto Samuel, Pray for thy servants unto the LORD thy God, that we die not: for we have added unto all our sins this evil, to ask us a king**. And Samuel said unto the people, <u>**Fear not: ye have done all this wickedness: yet turn not aside from following the LORD, but serve the LORD with all your heart**</u>; And turn ye not aside: for then should ye go after vain things, which cannot profit nor deliver; for they are vain. <u>For the LORD will not forsake his people for his great name's sake: because it hath pleased the LORD to make you his people.</u> Moreover as for me, God forbid that I should sin against the LORD in ceasing to pray for you: but I will teach you the good and the right way: **Only fear the LORD**, and serve him in truth with all your heart: for consider how great things he hath done for you. But if ye shall still do wickedly, ye shall be consumed, both ye and your king."*

This truly shows God's heart! **Fear not! God said even if you have sinned and now He brings forth judgment upon you, fear not.** You see, when God judges you, He doesn't do it to punish you or because you deserve it, because if that were the case, He would never send Jesus for us.

He does it to make us better. He judges His people or allows hard things to happen to them to make them better. Judgment is for our sake and if we know this, we won't fear Him even if we need to face the consequences of our actions, because we know that the end of a thing better than the beginning thereof.

If you are not strong enough to endure certain dealings or testing, God will keep you from it. 1 Corinthians 10:13 – *"There hath no temptation taken you but such as is common to man:* **but God is faithful, who will not suffer you to be tempted above that ye are able**; *but will with the temptation also make a way to escape, that ye may be able to bear it."* God doesn't allow just anything to happen in your life if you are faithfully walking with Him. So you don't need to fear. If He allows something to happen, He does it because He knows that you can endure it and at the end, it will edify you and make you better or stronger. So there is no reason to fear what comes upon you. He is in control.

God uses fear to judge, but that is not His first choice. Fear has a great power and He uses whatever He can to bring us back to Him, but again that is His last choice. God is Love. He draws us to Him with cords of love. But if we have a hardened and rebellious heart He has no choice. But even then, He does it so we would turn back to Him and see that there is peace and joy in His presence and outside of that, we would live in fear.

Chapter IX

Fear of the Enemy

The devil obviously wants us to be afraid of him, but the truth is he is sore afraid of God's people. We need to keep this in mind.

I. Examples of fear of the enemy

   A.   Exodus 14:13 – *"And Moses said unto the people, Fear ye not, stand still, and see the salvation of the LORD, which he will shew to you to day: for the Egyptians whom ye have seen to day, ye shall see them again no more for ever."*

Israel was afraid of Pharaoh's chariots at the Red Sea. They lacking in trust and faith in God. But look at the end what happened. They believed.

   B.   Deuteronomy 1:21,29 – *"Behold, the LORD thy God hath set the land before thee: go up and possess it, as the LORD God of thy fathers hath said unto thee;* **fear not***, neither be discouraged…Then I said unto you, Dread not,* **neither be afraid of them***."*

Israel was afraid to possess the promise land, afraid of the inhabitants of the promise land.

   C.   Deuteronomy 3:2 – *"And the LORD said unto me,* **Fear him not***: for I will deliver him, and all his people, and his land, into thy hand; and thou shalt do unto him as thou didst unto Sihon king of the Amorites, which dwelt at Heshbon."*

Israel was afraid of Og and his people.

   D.   Psalms 18:4 – *"The sorrows of death compassed me, and the* **floods of ungodly men made me afraid***."*

David was afraid of ungodly men.

   E.   Ezra 3:3 – *"And they set the altar upon his bases; for* **fear was upon them because of the people of those countries***: and they* offered burnt offerings thereon unto the LORD, even burnt offerings morning and evening."

F. 2 Samuel 17:2 – *"And **I will come upon him while he is weary** and weak handed, and will **make him afraid:** and all the people that are with him shall flee; and I will smite the king only."*

The enemy uses fear when we are weary and weak. "weary" = *tired*; hence (transitively) *tiresome* "weak" = *slack* (in body or mind) **Fear comes when we are weary, tired, and exhausted in our journey, and when we start slacking up!**

II. The enemy uses words to make you afraid

A. 2 Chronicles 32:7-8 – *"Be strong and courageous, <u>be not afraid nor dismayed</u> for the king of Assyria, nor for all the multitude that is with him: for there be more with us than with him: With him is an arm of flesh; but with us is the LORD our God to help us, and to fight our battles. And the people rested themselves upon the words of Hezekiah king of Judah."*

The king of Assyria made Israel afraid by using his words. verse 10-19! verse 18 – *"Then **they cried with a loud voice <u>in the Jews' speech</u>** unto the people of Jerusalem that were on the wall, **to affright them**, and to trouble them; that they might take the city."* The devil is like a roaring lion. He roars, he tries to affright us with his words, but the truth is that God is in control, and like an old lion who has no teeth or at least not too strong teeth, the enemy has no teeth anymore therefore the only thing he can use is his "roar" to scare us. Jesus overcame the enemy, so now it's on us that we listen to him and let fear overtake us or we decide to trust in God.

B. Psalms 64:1-10 – *"...Hide me from the secret counsel of the wicked; from the insurrection of the workers of iniquity: **Who whet their tongue like a sword**, and bend their bows to shoot their arrows, **even bitter words**: That they may shoot in secret at the perfect: suddenly do they shoot at him, and **fear not**..."*

The enemy uses their words to make us afraid. **They lie to us and use "bitter words"**.

C. Nehemiah 6:1-19 – *"Now it came to pass, when Sanballat, and Tobiah, and Geshem the Arabian, and the rest of our enemies, heard that I had builded the wall... That Sanballat and Geshem sent unto* me, **saying,** Come, let us meet together in some one of the villages in the plain of Ono. But they thought to do me mischief. And I sent messengers unto them, saying, I am doing a great work, so that I cannot come down... Then sent Sanballat his servant unto me in like manner the <u>fifth time</u> with an **open letter** in his hand... thou hast also appointed prophets to preach of thee at Jerusalem, saying, There is a king in Judah: and now shall it be reported to the king according to these words. Come now therefore, and let us take counsel together. Then I sent unto him, saying, **There are no such things done as thou sayest**, but thou feignest them out of thine own heart. For they all made us afraid, saying, Their hands shall be weakened from the work, that it be not done. Now therefore, O God, strengthen my hands. Afterward I came unto the house of Shemaiah the son of Delaiah the son of Mehetabeel, who was shut up; and he said, Let us meet together in the house of God, within the temple, and let us shut the doors of the temple: for they will come to slay thee; yea, in the night will they come to slay thee... And, lo, **I perceived that God had not sent him;** but that he pronounced this prophecy against me: for Tobiah and Sanballat had hired him. **Therefore was he hired, that I should be afraid, and do so, and sin**, and that they might have matter for an evil report, that they might reproach me. My God, think thou upon Tobiah and Sanballat according to these their works, and on the prophetess Noadiah, and the rest of the prophets, that would have put me in fear. So the wall was finished in the twenty and fifth day of the month Elul, in fifty and two days... And **Tobiah sent letters to put me in fear**."

This is a perfect example for how does the enemy use lying words to scare us, because fear can stop us to fulfill what God called us for. We can't listen to their words, just like Nehemiah and his men didn't.

D. 1 Samuel 17:11 – *"When Saul and all Israel **heard those words of the Philistine, they were dismayed, and greatly afraid.**"*

This is another great example for when the enemy uses lies to make us afraid which causes us to turn from our walk with God. Then the enemy can use our falling away against us. These are just lying words, and we need to *"perceive that God had not sent hi*m". The enemy will do everything to make you afraid and stop you from doing the will of God! Nehemiah was threatened multiple times just that he would stop the rebuilding of the temple. But **all was just a threat** to make him sin, or stop pressing on. **Most of the times the things we are so afraid of are just threats.**

III. We need to remember that the enemy fears God's people

God makes our enemy afraid of us so they will turn back and run from us.

A. Exodus 23:27 – "***I will send my fear before thee***, *and will destroy all the people to whom thou shalt come, and I will make all thine enemies turn their backs unto thee.*"
B. Esther 7:6 – "*And Esther said,* **The adversary** *and enemy is this wicked Haman. Then Haman* **was afraid before the king and the queen**."

C. 1 Samuel 18:12-15 – "***And Saul was afraid of David***, *because the LORD was with him, and was departed from Saul. Therefore Saul removed him from him, and made him his captain over a thousand; and he went out and came in before the people. And* **David behaved himself wisely** *in all his ways; and the LORD was with him.* **Wherefore** *when* **Saul** *saw that he behaved himself very wisely, he* **was afraid of him**."

This happened when Saul threw the javelin at David. He did it because he was afraid of him. In the mean time David was afraid of him:

1. 1 Samuel 21:10 – "*And David arose, and* **fled that day for fear of Saul**, *and went to Achish the king of Gath.*"
2. 1 Samuel 23:26 – "*And Saul went on this side of the mountain, and David and his men on that side of the mountain: and David* **made haste to get away for fear of Saul**; *for Saul and his men compassed David and his men round about to take them.*"

So many times we are so afraid of our enemies too, but the truth is they do all that to us because they themselves are afraid of us. **You see, our enemy will try to do anything to stop us from walking in God's way because he is AFRAID of us. Why should we be scared of him? If God is with us, then who can be against us?** Remember this next time when the enemy tries to make you afraid. We have no reason to fear because the King of kings, the Lord of lords is on our sides.

- D. Isaiah 19:16-17 - *"*^{16}*In that day shall **Egypt** be like unto women: and it **shall be afraid and fear** because of the shaking of the hand of the LORD of hosts, which he shaketh over it.* ^{17}*And **the land of Judah shall be a terror unto Egypt**, every one that maketh mention thereof shall be afraid in himself, because of the counsel of the LORD of hosts, which he hath determined against it."*

- E. 1Kings 1:49-50 - *"*^{49}*And **all the guests** that were with **Adonijah were afraid**, and rose up, and went every man his way.* ^{50}*And **Adonijah feared because of Solomon**, and arose, and went, and caught hold on the horns of the altar."*

Adonijah was afraid of Solomon. This happened after he tried to get the throne, but he didn't succeed.

- F. Genesis 35:5 - *"And they journeyed: and the **terror of God was upon the cities** that were round about them, and they did not pursue after the sons of Jacob."*

- G. Joshua 2:9-11 - *"*^{9}*And she said unto the men, I know that the LORD hath given you the land, and that **your terror is fallen upon us**, and that **all the inhabitants of the land faint because of you**.* ^{10}*For we have heard how the LORD dried up the water of the Red sea for you, when ye came out of Egypt; and what ye did unto the two kings of the Amorites, that were on the other side Jordan, Sihon and Og, whom ye utterly destroyed.* ^{11}*And as soon as we had heard these things, **our hearts did melt, neither did there remain any more courage in any man, because of you**: for the LORD your God, he is God in heaven above, and in earth beneath."*

Rahab was telling this to the two spies that Joshua sent to Jericho. The nations around them were greatly afraid of Israel because of what the Lord had done with the nations around them.

- H. Joshua 5:1 - *"And it came to pass, when **all the kings of the Amorites,** which were on the side of Jordan westward, and all the kings of the Canaanites, which were by the sea, heard that the LORD had dried up the waters of Jordan from before the children of Israel, until we were passed over, that **their heart melted, neither was there spirit in them any more, because of the children of Israel.**"*

- I. Mark 6:20 - *"For **Herod feared John, knowing that he was a just man and an holy**, and **observed him;** and when he heard him, he did many things, and heard him gladly."*
- J. 2 Samuel 9:7 – *"And David said unto him, Fear not: for I will surely shew thee kindness for Jonathan thy father's sake, and will restore thee all the land of Saul thy father; and thou shalt eat bread at my table continually."* – Mephibosheth was afraid of David.
- K. Revelation 11:11 - *"And after three days and an half the Spirit of life from God entered into them, and **they stood upon their feet; and great fear fell upon them which saw them**."*

This verse talks about the two witnesses that were dead, but after three and a half days God resurrected them. **The enemy may rejoice for a short time, thinking that they had victory over God's people, but that's just for a season and for a greater miracle.** In the end, all eyes will see the Glory of God and will tremble before His Presence and before His faithful servants.

IV. The Enemy Fears God

- A. Joshua 2:9 - *"And she said unto the men, I know that the LORD hath given you the land, and that your terror is fallen upon us, and that **all the inhabitants of the land faint because of you**."*

"Faint" = to *quiver* (with any violent emotion, especially anger or fear)

- B. Psalms 46:6 - *"The **heathen raged, the kingdoms were moved:** he uttered his voice, the earth melted."*

"Melt" = to *melt*, that is, literally (to *soften*, flow down, *disappear*), or figuratively (to *fear, faint*)

- C. Genesis 36:17 - *"And **these are the sons of Reuel Esau's son**; duke Nahath, duke Zerah, duke Shammah, duke **Mizzah**: these are the dukes that came of Reuel in the land of Edom; these are the sons of Bashemath Esau's wife."*

Mizzah was Esau's son, and Esau speaks of our fleshly nature. The name Mizzah means: to faint with fear, terror. It's no wonder we become so easily fearful in our flesh.

V. Babylon Will Fear God (At the Day of the Lord)

    A. Isaiah 13:8 - *"And they shall be afraid: pangs and sorrows shall take hold of them; they shall be in pain as a woman that travaileth: they shall be amazed one at another; their faces shall be as flames."*

    B. Jeremiah 50:2 - *"Declare ye among the nations, and publish, and set up a standard; publish, and conceal not: say, Babylon is taken, Bel is confounded, Merodach is* **broken in pieces**; *her idols are confounded, her images are broken in pieces."* – "broken pieces" means crushed, afraid, terror

VI. Ultimately All Creation Will Fear God's People:

    A. Genesis 9:2 – *"And* ***the fear of you and the dread of you shall be upon every beast of the earth,*** *and upon every fowl of the air, upon all that moveth upon the earth, and upon all the fishes of the sea; into your hand are they delivered."*

Chapter X

Other Types of Fear

I. Fear of sufferings for righteousness' sake

There are times when we need to suffer for righteousness sake, when God allows something in His wisdom that He could prevent in His power. God tries His people but we don't have to fear because *"we know that all things work together for good to them that love God, to them who are the called according to his purpose."* (Romans 8:28). God only asks us to be faithful unto death, because He will reward you with the crown of life.

- A. Job 31:23 – *"For **destruction from God was a terror to me**, and by reason of his highness I could not endure."*
- B. Revelation 2:9-10 *"⁹**I know thy works, and tribulation**, and poverty, (but thou art rich) and **I know the blasphemy** of them which say they are Jews, and are not, but are the synagogue . ¹⁰**Fear none of those things which thou shalt suffer**: behold, **the devil shall cast some of you into prison**, that ye may be tried; and **ye shall have tribulation ten days: be thou faithful unto death, and I will give thee a crown of life.**"*
- C. I Peter 3:14 *"But and **if ye suffer for righteousness' sake**, happy are ye: and **be not afraid of their terror, neither be troubled;**"*

II. Fear of the Multitudes

Numbers can easily intimidate us and can make us fearful, but with God is not about quantity but about quality. Leviticus 26:8 says *"And **five of you shall chase an hundred, and an hundred of you shall put ten***

thousand to flight*: and your enemies shall fall before you by the sword."* We don't need to fear because God's with us, then who can be against us. We need to remember that there are more with us than against us.

- A. 2 Chronicles 20:15, 17 – *"And he said, Hearken ye, all Judah, and ye inhabitants of Jerusalem, and thou king Jehoshaphat, Thus saith the LORD unto you,* **Be not afraid nor dismayed by reason of this great multitude**; <u>for the battle is not yours, but God's</u>... *Ye shall not need to fight in this battle: set yourselves, stand ye still, and see the salvation of the LORD with you, O Judah and Jerusalem: fear not, nor be dismayed; to morrow go out against them:* <u>for the LORD will be with you</u>.*"* Judah was afraid because the Moabites and the Ammonites were about to attack them. Their response was to fast and pray, then God answered them through prophecy and they worshiped.
- B. Deuteronomy 20:1 - *"When thou goest out to battle against thine enemies, and seest horses, and chariots, and a* **people more than thou, be not afraid of them**: <u>for the LORD thy God is with thee</u>, *which brought thee up out of the land of Egypt."* - Big numbers can be intimidating and can make us fearful, but God is with us so who can be against us.
- C. 2 Kings 6:15-17 *"¹⁵And when the servant of the man of God was risen early, and gone forth, behold, <u>an host compassed the city both with horses and chariots</u>. And his servant said unto him, Alas, my master! how shall we do? ¹⁶And he answered,* **Fear not: for they that be with us are more than they that be with them.** *¹⁷And Elisha prayed, and said, LORD, I pray thee, open his eyes, that he may see. And the LORD opened the eyes of the young man; and he saw: and, behold, the mountain was full of horses and chariots of fire round about Elisha."*

We need to remember that they that are with us are more than those who are against us!

- D. 1 Samuel 14:6 – *"and Jonathon said to the young man that bare his armor, Come, let us go over the garrison of these uncircumcised: it may be that the Lord will work for us: for there is no restraint to the Lord to save by many or by few."* - Jonathan had the revelation that numbers didn't matter to God. He can saved by few! Jonathan did not fear the multitude of people.

III. Fear From Family Members

Sometimes family members can be more intimidating than anybody else because they know us or think that they know us just because we grew up together. They also think that it gives them the right to judge us and to tell us what we should or shouldn't be doing. Matthew 13:57 says *"And they were offended in him. But Jesus said unto them, A **prophet is not without honour, save in his own country, and in his own house**."*

Sometimes the people closest to us persecute us the most. David was persecuted by his own son Absalom, and betrayed by the people closest to him. His brothers didn't take him seriously when he offered to fight Goliath, but it didn't stop him. Never forget that Jesus sticketh closer than a brother.

> A. Judges 6:27 – *"Then Gideon took ten men of his servants, and did as the LORD had said unto him: and so it was, because **he feared his father's household**, and the men of the city, that he could not do it by day, that he did it by night."*

Gideon feared his father and he feared Babylon. Because of his own father he was afraid to do the will of God and to destroy the altar of Baal. But in the end, he still did it.

> B. Judges 9:21 – *"And Jotham ran away, and fled, and went to Beer, and dwelt there, for **fear of Abimelech his brother**."*
>
> C. Acts 9:26 - *"And when Saul was come to Jerusalem, he assayed to join himself to the disciples: but **they were all afraid of him**, and believed not that he was a disciple."*

The disciples were afraid of Paul because what he had done. Also many of the Pharisees persecuted him, his own supposed brothers in God.

> D. Psalms 55:12-14 - *"¹²**For it was not an enemy that reproached me; then I could have borne it: neither was it he that hated me that did magnify himself against me**; then I would have hid myself from him: ¹³**But it was thou, a man mine equal, my guide, and mine acquaintance**. ¹⁴We took sweet counsel together, and walked unto the house of God in company."* - In the Scriptures David was despised and forsaken by those who were closest to him

E. Genesis 50:19-20 - *"And Joseph said unto them, **Fear not**: for am I in the place of God? ²⁰But as for you, ye thought evil against me; but God meant it unto good, to bring to pass, as it is this day, to save much people alive."* - Joseph's brothers were afraid that he would hurt them because of what they had done to him, but Joseph had mercy upon them. They had nothing to fear.

IV. Fear of Being Cursed

If we walk with God we don't need to be afraid of somebody cursing us or from witchcraft, because God is on our side and He will even turn the curse into blessing.

A. Deuteronomy 23:5 – *"Nevertheless the LORD thy God would not hearken unto Balaam; but the LORD thy God turned the curse into a blessing unto thee, because the LORD thy God loved thee."*

V. Fear of Idols, Demons or Other Creatures

A. Jeremiah 10:2, 5 – *"Thus saith the LORD, Learn not the way of the heathen, and **be not dismayed at the signs of heaven**; for the heathen are dismayed at them. They are upright as the palm tree, but speak not: they must needs be borne, because they cannot go. **Be not afraid** of them; **for they cannot do evil**, neither also is it in them to do good."*

Signs of heaven speak of astrology, superstitions, karma and the idols of the heathen etc. Signs also means appearing, so can also speak of any manifestation of any spiritual creatures like demons, or even angels or God Himself. Although, I think in this case, He is speaking about more about the monuments or idols erected by heathens, after the images of the heavenlies, like the moon god etc. I say this because the word sign also means appearing, monument, a signal as a flag etc. **Don't be moved by these kinds of things because they can't effect your life. No astrology or karma has anything to do with your life.** God is the only God and He is in control! Therefore instead of fearing these things, only fear God and walk in His commandments with your whole heart.

Chapter XI

Discouragement

So many things are out there to discourage us, but we should never be discouraged, but instead stand strong on the promises of God. Discouragement makes us fearful and that makes us disobey God's Word. Isaac was digging the well of his father that the Philistines stopped up, but the herdsmen strived with him. So he dug another one, and they took that one from him too. But then God appeared to him and said: *"I am the God of Abraham thy father:* **fear not***, for I am with thee, and will bless thee, and multiply thy seed for my servant Abraham's sake." (*Genesis 26:24). So he dug another one. He didn't give up even though he had a good reason to get discouraged and become fearful. But he did what God told him rather than murmuring like the Israelites did. Don't let discouragement make you fearful.

The word discourage in the Bible means: to be short, be impatient, be vexed, be grieved. It also means: to fear the consequences. It's so true that many times we get discouraged and stop doing what we know we should do, simply because we are afraid of the consequences.

I.   Because of the Way

   A.   Numbers 21:4 - *"And they journeyed from mount Hor by the way of the Red sea, to compass the land of Edom and* **the soul of the people was much discouraged because of the way***."*

Our walk with God is a long distance walk. We will get weary and tired "because of the way", but we should never be discouraged because God is always with us. Genesis 28:15 says this: *"And, behold, I am with thee, and will keep thee in all places whither thou goest, and will bring thee again into this land; for I will not leave thee, until I have done that which I have spoken to thee of."* He sees us through. He will keep us in all places whither we go, and will bring us again into this land. Be strong and don't let the length of the road discourage you.

Israel was so discouraged and started complaining. Then they sinned greatly against God and He sent the fiery serpents to destroy them. But even then, He prepared deliverance for them. Those who returned unto the Lord got healed. He never leaves us, never forsakes us. He never punishes us just for punishment's sake. Don't be impatient, just trust in God.

Like I said before, one of the meaning of the word discouragement is being impatient. When we walk on this long road with God after a while we start to become impatient and discouraged, but we can't let it to overcome us. We need to keep our eyes on God and on His promises. If we do that, we rest assured that He will be with us to keep us and to fulfill to all those He said to us.

II. Because of our Rebellion and Disobedience

    A.   Deuteronomy 1:21, 26 - *"Behold, the LORD thy God hath set the land before thee: **go up and possess it**, as the LORD God of thy fathers hath said unto thee; **fear not, neither be discouraged**... Notwithstanding ye would not go up, but **rebelled against the commandment of the LORD your God.**"*

Even though God commanded them to posses the land, they rebelled against the Word of God.

    1.   Numbers 13:20 - *"And what the land is, whether it be fat or lean, whether there be wood therein, or not. And **be ye of good courage**, and bring of the fruit of the land. Now the time was the time of the firstripe grapes."*

Fear and discouragement make us to disobey God's commandments. The opposite of this is true also. When we disobey God we become fearful. The meaning of the word "discouraged" in verse 21st means, to break down, either (literally) by violence, or (figuratively) by confusion and fear. The word "good courage" means to be strong, courageous, conquer, cleave, continue. God instructs us to continue, to conquer and be courageous and not let fear to hinder us obeying His Word. In this story we could see that Israelites did the exact opposite of what God told them to do. Don't follow their example.

III. Discouragement because of Others

Our own sisters and brothers can discourage us because of their disbelief. When people are afraid of something, many times they want to put that fear upon us too. But don't listen to their voices, only hear and obey God. **Don't let their lack of trust in God make you fearful and take you off the way God put you on.** Only Caleb and Joshua could enter into the promise land because they didn't let the opinion of others discourage them.

- A. Numbers 32:9 - *"For when they went up unto the valley of Eshcol, and saw the land, **they discouraged the heart of the children of Israel**, that they should not go into the land which the LORD had given them."*

Our brothers and sisters can stop us with their words to enter into the things God prepared for us. Don't let this to happen to you.

- B. Deuteronomy 1:28 - *"Whither shall we go up? **our brethren have discouraged our heart, saying, The people is greater and taller than we;** the cities are great and walled up to heaven; and moreover we have seen the sons of the Anakims there."*
- C. Isaiah 8:12 - *"Say ye not, A confederacy, to all them to whom this people shall say, A confederacy; **neither fear ye their fear, nor be afraid.**"* - We should not let the fear of others move us or make us fearful.
- D. Colossians 3:21 - *"Fathers, provoke not your children to anger, **lest they be discouraged**."*

"Discouraged" means in the Greek: to be disheartened, dispirited, broken in spirit. Fathers should encourage their children, like Paul, David and Moses did.

- 1. Deuteronomy 31:7 – *"And **Moses called unto Joshua**, and said unto him in the sight of all Israel, **Be strong and of a good courage**: for thou must go with this people unto the land which the LORD hath sworn unto their fathers to give them; and thou shalt cause them to inherit it."*
- 2. 1 Chronicles 28:20 – *"And **David said to Solomon** his son, **Be strong and of good courage**, and do it: **fear not, nor be dismayed**: for the LORD God, even my God, will be with thee; he will not fail thee, nor forsake thee, until thou hast finished all the work for the service of the house of the LORD."*
- 3. 2 Timothy 1:2-14 – *"**To Timothy, my dearly beloved son**: Grace, mercy, and peace, from God the Father and Christ Jesus our Lord. I thank God, whom I serve from my forefathers with pure conscience, that without ceasing I have remembrance of thee in my prayers night and day..."*

III. The Word of God exhorts us to be of good courage and to not be discouraged

"Good courage" in the Hebrew means: to be strong, alert, courageous, to be determined, persist in. We should be encouraging each other.

   A. God's encouragement against the fear of the enemy

God's Word is full of promises saying that He will take care of our enemies if we obey His commandments.

   1. Deuteronomy 20:1-3 - *"¹When thou goest out to battle against thine enemies, and seest horses, and chariots, and a people more than thou, **be not afraid of them**: for the LORD thy God is with thee, which brought thee up out of the land of Egypt. ²And it shall be, when ye are come nigh unto the battle, that the priest shall approach and speak unto the people, ³And shall say unto them, Hear, O Israel, ye approach this day unto battle against your enemies: **let not your hearts faint, fear not, and do not tremble, neither be ye terrified because of them.**"*
   2. Leviticus 26:6 - *"And I will give peace in the land, and ye shall lie down, and **none shall make you afraid**: and I will rid evil beasts out of the land, neither shall the sword go through your land."*
   3. Jeremiah 30:10-11 - *"¹⁰Therefore **fear thou not**, O my servant Jacob, saith the LORD; neither be dismayed, O Israel: for, lo, **I will save thee from afar**, and thy seed from the land of their captivity; and Jacob shall return, and shall be in rest, and be quiet, **and none shall make him afraid**. ¹¹For I am with thee, saith the LORD, to save thee: though I make a full end of all nations whither I have scattered thee, yet will I not make a full end of thee: but I will correct thee in measure, and will not leave thee altogether unpunished."*
   4. Luke 10:19 - *"Behold, I give unto you power to tread on serpents and scorpions, and over all the power of the enemy: and nothing shall by any means hurt you."*
   5. Deuteronomy 7:21 - *"**Thou shalt not be affrighted at them: for the LORD thy God is among you, a mighty God and terrible.**"*
   6. 1 Peter 5:8-10 - *"⁸Be sober, be vigilant; because your adversary **the devil, as a roaring lion, walketh about, seeking whom he may devour**: ⁹Whom resist stedfast in the faith, knowing*

that the same afflictions are accomplished in your brethren that are in the world. ¹⁰*But* **the God of all grace***, who hath called us unto his eternal glory by Christ Jesus, after that ye have suffered a while,* **make you perfect, stablish, strengthen, settle you.**"

7. Psalms 17:4 - "*Concerning the works of men,* ***by the word of thy lips I have kept me from the paths of the destroyer.***"

8. 1 Samuel 2:10 – "***The adversaries of the LORD shall be broken*** *to pieces; out of heaven shall he thunder upon them: the LORD shall judge the ends of the earth; and* ***he shall give strength unto his king, and exalt the horn of his anointed.***"

9. Jeremiah 50:2 – "*Declare ye among the nations, and publish, and set up a standard; publish, and conceal not: say, Babylon is taken, Bel is confounded, Merodach is broken in pieces; her idols are confounded, her images are broken in pieces.*" - The enemies of God will be broken down in fear, but He shall give strength to His kings.

   a) Isaiah 30:31 – "*For through the voice of the Lord shall the Assyrian be beaten down, which smote with a rod.*"

B. Man of God ought to encourage his fellow saints to not be afraid

We need to encourage, build up each other, and if we do that the enemy can't prevail over us and we can have victory.

1. Joshua 10:25 – "*And Joshua said unto them,* ***Fear not, nor be dismayed, be strong and of good courage****: for thus shall the LORD do to all your enemies against whom ye fight.*"

Joshua encouraged the Israelites not to be afraid from the enemy. Joshua comforted Israel with the same comfort with which God had comforted him. (2 Corinthians 1:4 - "*Who comforteth us in all our tribulation, that we may be able to comfort them which are in any trouble, by the comfort wherewith we ourselves are comforted of God.*")

2. 1 Chronicles 22:13 – "*Then shalt thou prosper, if thou takest heed to fulfil the statutes and judgments which the LORD charged Moses with concerning Israel:* ***be strong, and of good courage; dread not, nor be dismayed.***" – And here David encourages Solomon.

3. 1 Chronicles 28:20 – *"And David said to Solomon his son, **Be strong and of good courage, and do it: fear not, nor be dismayed**: for the LORD God, even my God, will be with thee; he will not fail thee, nor forsake thee, until thou hast finished all the work for the service of the house of the LORD"* - David

4. Romans 8:15 - *"For **ye have not received the spirit of bondage again to fear; but ye have received the Spirit of adoption**, whereby we cry, Abba, Father."*

Paul exhorts us with this verse. A good father in God is with us even in fear. (1 Corinthians 2:3 - *"And I was with you in weakness, and in fear, and in much trembling."*) He can encourage them out of his own experiences.

5. Deuteronomy 31:6-8 - *"⁶Be **strong and of a good courage, fear not**, nor be afraid of them: for the LORD thy God, he it is that doth go with thee; he will not fail thee, nor forsake thee. ⁷And Moses called unto Joshua, and said unto him in the sight of all Israel, **Be strong and of a good courage**: for thou must go with this people unto the land which the LORD hath sworn unto their fathers to give them; and thou shalt cause them to inherit it. ⁸And the LORD, he it is that doth go before thee; he will be with thee, he will not fail thee, neither forsake thee: fear not, neither be dismayed."*

6. Joshua 1:9 - *"**Have not I commanded thee? Be strong and of a good courage; be not afraid**, neither be thou dismayed: for the LORD thy God is with thee whithersoever thou goest."* – Here God encourages Joshua.

7. 2 Samuel 10:12 - *"Be **of good courage**, and let us play the men for our people, and for the cities of our God: and the LORD do that which seemeth him good."* (1 Chronicles 19:13 *"**Be of good courage**, and let us behave ourselves valiantly for our people, and for the cities of our God: and let the LORD do that which is good in his sight."*)

Joab encourages his son and the army of Israel. We should encourage each other as they did. <u>It is God's commandment</u>!

8. Ezra 10:4 - *"Arise; for this matter belongeth unto thee: we also will be with thee: **be of good courage, and do it.**"*

Ezra was weeping and praying to God because of the multitude of sins of the people. Shechaniah encourages Ezra that even though Israel sinned by taking strange wives to themselves "*yet now there is hope in Israel concerning this thing*" because they will leave their wives willingly. So he told to Ezra to get up and do what he needs to do and he and the people will be behind him in this thing.

9. Psalms 27:14 - "**Wait on the LORD: be of good courage**, *and he shall strengthen thine heart: wait, I say, on the LORD.*"
10. Psalms 31:24 - "**Be of good courage**, *and he shall strengthen your heart, all ye that hope in the LORD.*" – Here David encourages himself and all of us.
11. Deuteronomy 1:21 – "*Behold, the LORD thy God hath set the land before thee: go up and possess it, as the LORD God of thy fathers hath said unto thee;* **fear not, neither be discouraged**."
12. Exodus 14:13 – "*And Moses said unto the people,* **Fear ye not, stand still**, *and see the salvation of the LORD, which he will shew to you to day: for the Egyptians whom ye have seen to day, ye shall see them again no more for ever. The LORD shall fight for you, and ye shall hold your peace.*"

In this passage Moses encouraged Israel with reminding them what a great things God has done for them already. How He brought them out of Egypt, and that He never forsake them. They were complaining because they were full of fear of the enemy and death.

13. Deuteronomy 20:1-4 – "*When thou goest out to battle against thine enemies, and seest horses, and chariots, and a people more than thou, be not afraid of them: for the LORD thy God is with thee, which brought thee up out of the land of Egypt. And it shall be,* **when ye are come nigh unto the battle, that the priest shall** *approach and speak unto the people, And shall* **say unto them**, *Hear, O Israel, ye approach this day unto battle against your enemies:* **let not your hearts faint, fear not, and do not tremble, neither be ye terrified because of them**; *For the LORD your God is he that goeth with you, to fight for you against your enemies, to save you.*"

The ministry of the priest is to encourage the people who are ready to go out to "battle". **Our ministry is to encourage each other in our daily battles.**

> 14. Philippians 1:14 - *"And many of the brethren in the Lord, waxing confident by my bonds, are much more bold to speak the word without fear."*

People became more confident in sharing the message of Jesus by witnessing Paul's afflictions. The way we live our lives can encourage the people around us to do the same. **Paul's disciples became bold and without fear after they witnessed their father's fearless confidence.**

> 15. 1 Samuel 23:16-18 – *And Jonathan Saul's son arose, and went to David into the wood, and strengthened his hand in God. And he said unto him, Fear not: for the hand of Saul my father shall not find thee; and thou shalt be king over Israel, and I shall be next unto thee; and that also Saul my father knoweth. And they two made a covenant before the LORD: and David abode in the wood, and Jonathan went to his house."*

David was running from Saul, but Jonathan went out and encouraged him in God. We need each other in our greatest times of distress.

IV. Examples of those who were encouraged by none other than God during their hardships.

There are times when there is nobody near to encourage us or to give strength to face the things before us. Sometimes God separates us for a season to teach how to find encouragement in Him, and that we would go to him first, before anybody else, and to learn to lean on Him rather than ourselves or other men. Like I said before, we definitely need to encourage each other, still God's highest will is to find encouragement, strength and courage in Him.

David and Jesus were left alone in the time of their great trials, but they were not alone, for the Father was with them. They encouraged themselves in the Lord.

> A. David – 1 Samuel 30:6 – *"And David was greatly distressed; for the people spoke of stoning him, because the soul of all the people was*

grieved, every man for his sons and for his daughters: but David encouraged himself in the Lord his God."
  B. Jesus – John 16:32 – *"Behold, the hour cometh, yea, is now come, that ye shall be scattered, every man to his own, and shall leave me alone: and yet I am not alone, because the Father is with me."*

We may think that we're alone, but we are not alone, *"He knoweth the way I take"*. In the end, God is our ultimate answer for our discouragement.

Chapter XII

What to do when we fear?

2 Chronicles 20:12-17 says *"O our God, wilt thou not judge them? for we have no might against this great company that cometh against us;* **neither know we what to do: but our eyes are upon thee....**" - Sometimes when fear arises we don't know what to do, but that's the key; we need to keep our eyes on Jesus and not our own strength and one thing is for sure; we should never go and seek the counsel of the ungodly. Psalms 1:1 *"Blessed is the man that walketh not in the counsel of the ungodly..."*

I. What fear does to you if you don't trust God and don't wait for Him

   A. 1 Samuel 28:5-7 – *"And **when Saul saw the host of the Philistines, he was afraid**, and his heart greatly trembled. And when Saul enquired of the LORD, the LORD answered him not, neither by dreams, nor by Urim, nor by prophets. **Then said Saul unto his servants, Seek me a woman that hath a familiar spirit, that I may go to her, and enquire of her**. And his servants said to him, Behold, there is a woman that hath a familiar spirit at Endor."*

This is a great example of what fear, and disobedience, and pride all together can make you do. Fear can make us do things that otherwise we wouldn't even dream of doing it.

   B. 2 Kings 25:26 – *"**And all the people**, both small and great, and the captains of the armies, arose, and **came to Egypt: for they were afraid** of the Chaldees."*

Israel fled to Egypt because they were afraid. This is not the first time they fled to Egypt.
Fear makes us run to the flesh rather than to God. We try to find deliverance in the natural. We try to "fix" the situation rather than stand still and wait for the salvation of the Lord like Moses instructed God's people (Exodus 14:13)

If we want to be free from fear, then first and foremost, we need to get to know God and His character. He is our foundation. We can't build upon anything else but Him. Everything is standing on the character of God! Times change and seasons change, but God's character never changes. So if we know Him, we will never be moved. Knowing who He is will be the anchor of our soul. Knowing Him is our stronghold, where we can run anytime we are afraid, until the storm passes. Knowing Him will keep us. He is the only thing that never changes. God will not change and we can take great comfort in that. The way He deals with us may change season to season, but He will never change, and that's what we can hold on to. Knowing His precious character keeps us in the storm. We can make it through anything if we just hold on to Him, His name, and His character.

The Bible says: *"But the LORD your God ye shall fear; and he shall deliver you out of the hand of all your enemies."* (2 Kings 17:39). It is pretty simple isn't it? But what does it really mean to fear God? Surely it doesn't mean that we need to be scared of Him. Fearing God is to have such a great reverence for Him that we want to follow His commandments, we want to obey Him in everything and we utterly trust His name and His character. Also, Proverbs 2:2-5 says: *"²So that thou **incline thine ear unto wisdom**, and **apply thine heart to understanding**; ³Yea, **if thou criest after knowledge**, and liftest up thy voice for understanding; ⁴**If thou seekest her as silver**, and searchest for her as for hid treasures; ⁵**Then shalt thou understand the fear of the LORD**, and find the knowledge of God."* Then Proverbs 8:13 says, **"The fear of the LORD is to hate evil: pride, and arrogancy, and the evil way, and the froward mouth, do I hate."** So, if we fear God, we do our best to cast all these things that God hates away from us at whatever cost. We need to try our best to die daily to all our ungodly, fleshly desires and apply our hearts to understanding, because the Truth (the Word of God, Jesus) makes us free. Therefore, we don't need to fear, for He will deliver us out of the hand of our enemies. Hallelujah! Thank you precious Jesus for your sacrifice!

II. What do we need to do when we fear?

    A. Be taught of God and eat up His Word

God's Word makes us free from fear. We find comfort, encouragement in it and we get to know God through it. And if we know God then we realize we have nothing to fear, because if God with us, who can be against us. If we fill ourselves with the Word of God we start listening His Words rather than the words that makes us afraid.

        1. Ezekiel 3:3 - *"And he said unto me, Son of man, **cause thy belly to eat, and fill thy bowels with this roll** that I give*

thee. Then did I eat it; and it was in my mouth as honey for sweetness."

Ezekiel was afraid to speak to the people the truth, but God told him to eat His word then go. God told him in Ezekiel 2:6 that *"be not afraid of them, neither be afraid of their words"* and in Ezekiel 3 He tells him to go and eat His words. So Ezekiel "ate" the Word, then he went and told the people what God instructed them to do. The Word of God delivers us from fear. It is a powerful weapon in our mouth.

2. Isaiah 54:13-14 - *"¹³And all **thy children shall be taught of the LORD**; and great shall be the peace of thy children. ¹⁴In righteousness shalt thou be established: thou shalt be far from oppression; for **thou shalt not fear: and from terror**; for it shall not come near thee."*

If we be taught of the Lord we will have peace, because we will know the truth and the lying words of the enemy can't overpower us anymore.

3. Proverbs 3:21, 24-25 - *"²¹My son, let not them depart from thine eyes: **keep sound wisdom** and discretion...²⁴When thou liest down, **thou shalt not be afraid**: yea, thou shalt lie down, and thy sleep shall be sweet. ²⁵**Be not afraid of sudden fear**, neither of the desolation of the wicked, when it cometh."*

4. Song of Solomon 3:8 - *"**They all hold swords**, being expert in war: every man hath his sword upon his thigh **because of fear in the night**."*

The Bible compares the Word of God to a two edged sword. Hebrews 4:12 - *"For the word of God is quick, and powerful, and sharper than any twoedged sword, piercing even to the dividing asunder of soul and spirit, and of the joints and marrow, and is a discerner of the thoughts and intents of the heart.*

5. Jeremiah 23:4 – *"And I **will set up shepherds over them which shall feed them: and they shall fear no more**, nor be dismayed, neither shall they be lacking, saith the LORD."*

One of the most important duty of the pastor of a congregation is to feed the sheep with God's Word. If they do that they will fear no more and they won't be lacking. God's Word will keep them from the destroyer.

B. Simply call upon His name

This seems very obvious, yet many turn to others for help rather than God. Just like we saw in the case of Adam and Eve. They hide themselves and tried to covered themselves with leaves rather than run to God. Never forget that doesn't matter what kind of situation we're in or what we've done, we could never go wrong by calling God for our aid. We simply need to call upon His name. The only time He doesn't hear our voice if we continue to be stiff necked and rebellious. In that case, He needs to prove us first, and then He will listen to our cry. Therefore don't hesitate to call upon God when you are afraid!

1. Psalms 18:6 - "***In my distress I called upon the LORD***, *and cried unto my God: he heard my voice out of his temple, and my cry came before him, even into his ears.*"
2. 2 Samuel 22:5,7 - "***When*** *the waves of death compassed me,* ***the floods of ungodly men made me afraid***...*In my distress* ***I called upon the LORD, and cried to my God****: and he did hear my voice out of his temple, and my cry did enter into his ears.*"
3. Judges 2:18 - "*And when the LORD raised them up judges, then the* ***LORD was with the judge, and delivered them out of the hand of their enemies*** *all the days of the judge: for it repented the LORD* ***because of their groanings by reason of them that oppressed them*** *and vexed them.*"
4. Exodus 2:23-25 "*²³And it came to pass in process of time, that the king of Egypt died: and the children of* ***Israel sighed by reason of the bondage, and they cried, and their cry came up unto God by reason of the bondage.*** *²⁴**And God heard their groaning, and God remembered his covenant with Abraham, with Isaac, and with Jacob***. *And God looked upon the children of Israel, and* ***God had respect unto them****.*" - Isn't that precious? God respected them. Thank you for your kindness Jesus!
5. Job 34:28 "*So that they cause the cry of the poor to come unto him, and* ***he heareth the cry of the afflicted****.*"

C. Worship Him

Worship and praise brings the presence of God, and where light is, there is no darkness. The word presence means face to face, the face (as the part that turns). Worship brings the presence of God. When we worship God He turns His face towards us and we can see Him face to face us and where the Light is, darkness must flee.

1. 1 Samuel 16:14,16 - *"But the Spirit of the LORD departed from Saul, and an **evil spirit from the LORD troubled him**.... Let our lord now command thy servants, which are before thee, to seek out a man, who is a cunning player on an harp: and it shall come to pass, **when the evil spirit from God is upon thee, that he shall play with his hand, and thou shalt be well**."*
2. Psalms 34:4 - *"I <u>**sought**</u> the LORD, and he heard me, and **delivered me from all my fears**."*

   a. "Sought" - To tread or frequent, usually <u>to follow</u> (for pursuit or search); by implication to seek or ask; specifically <u>to worship</u>

D. Remember what He has done for us

We need to remind ourselves to all those things that God has done for us, instead of listening the lying words of the enemy. If God has done for us in the past, He can do it in the present. He never changes.

1. Deuteronomy 7:17-19 - *"¹⁷If thou shalt say in thine heart, These nations are more than I; how can I dispossess them? ¹⁸**Thou shalt not be afraid of them**: but **shalt well remember what the LORD thy God did unto Pharaoh, and unto all Egypt**; ¹⁹The great temptations which thine eyes saw, and the signs, and the **wonders, and the mighty hand**, and the **stretched out arm**, whereby the LORD thy God brought thee out: **so shall the LORD thy God do unto all the people of whom thou art afraid**."*
2. Deuteronomy 1:29-32 - *"²⁹Then I said unto you, **Dread not, neither be afraid of them**. ³⁰The LORD your God which goeth before you, he shall fight for you, **according to all that he did for you in Egypt before your eyes**; ³¹**And in the wilderness**, where thou hast seen how that the LORD thy God bare thee, as a man doth bear his son, in all the way that ye went, until ye came into this place. ³²Yet in this thing ye did not believe the LORD your God."*

3. Hebrews 11:21 - *"By faith Jacob, when he was a dying, blessed both the sons of Joseph; and worshipped, leaning upon the top of his staff."*

People marked what they went through in their lives on their staff. So leaning upon a staff also means that we are leaning on our experiences: God's deliverance and His faithfulness to us in those times. You need to lean upon what God has done for you and then you will find the strength to not only continue and finish your journey strong, but bless people in the midst of it. Remember Him and put all things to your remembrance that he has done for you!

E. With perfection, fear will be wiped away

The day when we stop doing iniquity, when we will be established in righteousness, that day will nothing can make us afraid. This is the consequences of walking with God, of being perfect or being complete. This is when we fulfill all the things that God prepared for us from the beginning of time.

1. Zephaniah 3:13 - *"**The remnant of Israel shall not do iniquity**, nor speak lies; neither shall a deceitful tongue be found in their mouth: for they shall feed and lie down, **and none shall make them afraid**."*
2. Isaiah 54:14 - *"In **righteousness shalt thou be established**: thou shalt be far from oppression; for **thou shalt not fear**: and from terror; for it shall not come near thee."*
3. Job 11:13 – *"If thou **prepare thine heart**, and stretch out thine hands toward him; **If iniquity be in thine hand, put it far away**, and let not wickedness dwell in thy tabernacles. For then **shalt thou lift up thy face without spot**; yea, thou shalt be stedfast, and **shalt not fear**... Also thou shalt lie down, and none shall make thee afraid..."*

We **need to repent** from all of our sins, and let the word of God wash our hearts thoroughly.

F. If we are free from condemnation, we are free from fear

1 John 3:21 says, *"Beloved, **if our heart condemn us not**, then have **we confidence toward God**."* The word "confidence" in the Greek means: **Free and fearless confidence**, cheerful courage, boldness, all out spokenness,

frankness, bluntness. Condemnation robs you from the fearless confidence and cheerful courage of God. The first step to becoming fearless is to not let our heart to condemn us. Only God can help us, but if we distance ourselves from God with condemnation and we don't trust Him, sooner or later fear will arise in our hearts.

    G.   Be in His presence

God presence casts out all fear. Therefore if we dwell with God, we have nothing to fear of. Psalms 91:1,5 says, "*¹**He that dwelleth in the secret place of the most High** shall abide under the shadow of the Almighty...⁵thou **shalt not be afraid** for the terror by night; nor for the arrow that flieth by day;*"

Then we can read in Psalms 23:4, *"Yea, though I walk through the valley of the shadow of death, **I will fear no evil: for thou art with me; thy rod and thy staff they comfort me.**"* The word "rod" in the Hebrew means a stick used for punishing, writing, fighting, ruling, correction, but the word staff means support, sustenance. Rod is for guidance and the staff is for our support. God corrects us and lead us by His rod, which is His Word. His rod also gives us authority and power. **If we have the presence of God, the Word of God, and support and comfort of the Holy Spirit, we will not fear anything**, even if we walk through the valley of shadow of death.

    H.   Obey Him

God promised to us that if we obey Him and keep His commandments, we have nothing to fear. God said in Leviticus 26:1-3, 6, *"...³**If ye walk in my statutes, and keep my commandments, and do them**... ⁶And I will give peace in the land, and ye shall lie down, and **none shall make you afraid**: and I will rid evil beasts out of the land, neither shall the sword go through your land."* We need to obey God and keep His commandments and He will give peace and life without fear.

Proverbs 1:33 says, *"But **whoso hearkeneth unto me** shall dwell safely, and **shall be quiet from fear of evil**."* The world "Hearkeneth" doesn't only mean to hear and listen to, but also to **obey**. **This means that we not only hear what God says but we obey Him, we act upon that word**. It means we are hearing with the intention of doing that word, with the intention of being obedient.

I know it's easier said then done. This is not that simple. Even Jesus learned obedience through sufferings (Hebrews 5:8). We need to go through times of sufferings also so we will learn to be obedient to God in all things and our will is no longer ours, but God's. Jesus reached this point at the end of His life. **(***"Not my will but thine be done"***) Once you reach that point, you will no longer fear the enemy. You will become fearless.** Thank you Jesus!

I. Watch and be sober

1 Peter 5:8 instructs us to *"****Be sober,*** *be vigilant; because your adversary the devil, as a* ***roaring lion****, walketh about, seeking whom he may devour."* Satan is not only a crouching lion or a lion that stealthfully creeps towards his prey, but he is a roaring lion who, by his terrible roar, tries to intimidate us so that we might become easy prey. **Fear is just the roar of a lion**. Satan **wants to scare you and intimidate you so that you lose you're your confidence in God.** Therefore be sober! Be vigilant! Don't let the roar, the shadow intimidate you! Put your confidence in God. Trust in God!

J. Abide in a God appointed place for you

1 Chronicles 17:9 says that God appointed a place for Israel, where He keeps them safe. *"Also I will ordain a place for my people Israel, and will plant them, and* ***they shall dwell in their place****, and* ***shall be moved no more****; neither shall the children of wickedness waste them any more, as at the beginning,"* The word "Move" also means t**o** ***quiver*** (with any violent emotion, especially anger or **fear**). Therefore if we won't leave the place that God appointed for us, we won't be moved wit fear either.

K. Pray & Fast

Few examples of God's people praying when they were afraid of the enemy.

1. Jeremiah 17:18 – *"Let them be confounded that persecute me, but let not me be confounded: let them* ***be dismayed,*** *but let not me be dismayed: bring upon them the day of evil, and destroy them with double destruction"* – Jeremiah's prayer to God.
2. Psalms 64:1-10 – *"Hear my voice, O God, in my prayer:* ***preserve my life from fear of the enemy****.* ***Hide me from the secret counsel of the wicked****; from the insurrection of the workers of iniquity: Who whet their tongue like a sword, and bend their bows to shoot their arrows, even bitter words: That*

> they may shoot in secret at the perfect: suddenly do they shoot at him, and fear not. They encourage themselves in an evil matter: they commune of laying snares privily; they say, Who shall see them? They search out iniquities; they accomplish a diligent search: both the inward thought of every one of them, and the heart, is deep. **But God shall shoot at them with an arrow; suddenly shall they be wounded. So they shall make their own tongue to fall upon themselves: all that see them shall flee away. And all men shall fear, and shall declare the work of God; for they shall wisely consider of his doing.** The righteous shall be glad in the LORD, and shall trust in him; and all the upright in heart shall glory."

David prayed this when he was afraid because of the lies of the enemy. This is a great prayer when we are in fear because of the lies of the enemy.

    3.   2 Chronicles 20:2-3 – "*Then there came some that told Jehoshaphat, saying, There cometh a great multitude against thee from beyond the sea on this side Syria; and, behold, they be in Hazazontamar, which is Engedi.* **And Jehoshaphat feared, and set himself to seek the LORD, and proclaimed a fast throughout all Judah.**"

  L.   We can be comforted by the love of others

2 Corinthians 7:5-7 says that "*⁵For, when we were come into Macedonia, our flesh had no rest, but we were troubled on every side; <u>without were fightings</u>,* **within were fears**. *⁶Nevertheless God, that comforteth those that are cast down,* **comforted us by** *the coming of* **Titus**; *⁷And not by his coming only, but by the consolation wherewith he was* **comforted in you**, *when he told us your earnest desire, your mourning, your fervent mind toward me; so that I rejoiced the more.*" Paul had fears within, but God comforted them through other disciples and their fruits. When we have fear within, we can be comforted by the love of others and the longing that they have towards us. This is why important that the love of God dwell within us and to love one another, with that we can help those that fight with fear. John 13:35 says, that "*By this shall all men know that ye are my disciples, if ye have love one to another.*" God's children love one other and help each other. The devil doesn't want that we stand in unity against him, because then nobody can stop us.

  M.   Stir up God's gifts within you

Paul said in 2 Timothy 1:6-7 - *"⁶Wherefore I put thee in remembrance that thou **stir up the gift of God**, which is in thee by the putting on of my hands. ⁷**For God hath not given us the spirit of fear; but of power**, and of love, and of a sound mind."* The word fear in the Greek means *timidity*. We have no reason to be timid, we just need to remember what's inside of us. Teh Spirit of love and power.

But how do we stir ourselves up? We need to remember what God has already done for us.

1. 2 Peter 1:13 - *"Yea, I think it meet, as long as I am in this tabernacle, **to stir you up by putting you in remembrance**."*
2. 2 Peter 3:1 - *"This second epistle, beloved, I now write unto you; in both which **I stir up your pure minds by way of remembrance**."*

N. We need to remember that our God, who has created both good and evil, is in control

Isaiah 54:16-17 says, *"¹⁶Behold, I have created the smith that bloweth the coals in the fire, and that bringeth forth an instrument for his work; and I have created the waster to destroy. ¹⁷No **weapon that is formed against thee shall prosper**; and every tongue that shall rise against thee in judgment thou shalt condemn. This is the heritage of the servants of the LORD, and their righteousness is of me, saith the LORD."* God is in control. We don't need to be scared because He is the all-knowing, forever merciful God who created even the evil to destroy, and He is on our side.

He also assured of this: *"⁷For a small moment have I forsaken thee; **but** with great mercies will I gather thee. ⁸In a little wrath I hid my face from thee for a moment; **but** with everlasting kindness will I have mercy on thee, saith the LORD thy Redeemer."* (Isaiah 54:7-8)

Chapter XIII

Above All...

I. **Above all, we need to tell ourselves not to be afraid for God is for us and He is with us.**

   A. Psalms 27:1-3 - *"¹A Psalm of David.* **The LORD is my light and my salvation; whom shall I fear?** *the LORD is the strength of my life;* **of whom shall I be afraid?** *²When the wicked, even mine enemies and my foes, came upon me to eat up my flesh, they stumbled and fell. ³Though an host should encamp against me,* **my heart shall not fear***: though war should rise against me, in this will I be confident."*
   B. Isaiah 12:2 - *"Behold,* **God is my salvation; I will trust, and not be afraid***: for the LORD JEHOVAH is my strength and my song; he also is become my salvation."*
   C. Psalms 118:1-13 - *"O* **give thanks unto the LORD***; for he is good: because his mercy endureth for ever.* **Let Israel now say, that his mercy endureth for ever***. Let the house of Aaron now say, that his mercy endureth for ever.* **Let them now that fear the LORD say, that his mercy endureth for ever***. I called upon the LORD in distress: the LORD answered me, and set me in a large place.* **The LORD is on my side; I will not fear: what can man do unto me?***... It is better to trust in the LORD than to put confidence in man... Thou hast thrust sore at me that I might fall: but the LORD helped me."*

We don't need to fear because His mercy endureth for ever for Israel, for Aaron's family, for those who give thanks to God, and for all those who fear the Lord. The Lord is on our side! Like Psalms 23:4 says *"Yea, though I walk through the valley of the shadow of death, I will fear no evil:* **for thou art with me;** *thy rod and thy staff they comfort me."*

II. **God commands us not to fear**

This is God's commandment. Therefore we need to take it seriously. Fear not!

A. Joshua 1:9 – *"**Have not I commanded thee?** Be strong and of a good courage; **be not afraid**, neither be thou dismayed: **for the LORD thy God is with thee whithersoever thou goest**."*

B. Joshua 8:1 – *"And the LORD said unto Joshua, **Fear not, neither be thou dismayed**: take all the people of war with thee, and arise, go up to Ai: see, I have given into thy hand the king of Ai, and his people, and his city, and his land:"*

III. **Reasons why fear comes**

    A. Unbelief

        1. Exodus 14:11-14 – *"And they said unto Moses, Because there were no graves in Egypt, hast thou taken us away to die in the wilderness? wherefore hast thou dealt thus with us, to carry us forth out of Egypt? Is not this the word that we did tell thee in Egypt, saying, **Let us alone, that we may serve the Egyptians? For it had been better for us to serve the Egyptians, than that we should die in the wilderness**. And Moses said unto the people, **Fear ye not, stand still, and see the salvation of the LORD, which he will shew to you to day: for the Egyptians whom ye have seen to day, ye shall see them again no more for ever**. The LORD shall fight for you, and ye shall hold your peace."*

Israel was afraid of the Egyptians, because they did not believe and trust God. When we don't believe in God and in His Word, fear arises in our hearts. But if we trust Him, faith arises liek we saw in verse 31. (Exodus 14:31 - *"And Israel saw that great work which the LORD did upon the Egyptians: and the people feared the LORD, and **believed the LORD**, and his servant Moses."*)

        2. Numbers 14:9 – *"Only rebel not ye against the LORD, neither fear ye the people of the land; for they are bread for us: their defence is departed from them, and the LORD is with us: fear them not."*

Rebellion against God goes hand in hand with fear.

        3. Mark 5:36 – *"…Be not afraid, only believe."* – Jesus said it!

Fear and doubt are tied together just like faith and life without fear.

B. Disobedience

    1. Jeremiah 8:9 – *"The wise men are ashamed, **they are dismayed and taken**: lo, they have rejected the word of the LORD; and what wisdom is in them?"*

        a. "Dismay" means - Break down by confusion and fear.

If you reject the word of God, fear will arise in your heart and you will "break down in confusion and fear".

    2. Jeremiah 1:17 – *"Thou therefore gird up thy loins, and arise, and **speak unto them all that I command thee**: be not dismayed at their faces, **lest I confound thee before them**."*

God commands Jeremiah here to do what He asked him to do, because if he won't God will make Jeremiah afraid. God commands us not to disobey His Word because of fear of the enemy. If we do, <u>He</u> said that He will make us afraid of them.

IV. What God will do with the enemy and the Gentiles

    A. Jeremiah 46:1, 5 - *"**The word of the LORD** which came to Jeremiah the prophet **against the Gentiles**... Wherefore **have I seen them dismayed and turned away back**? and **their mighty ones are beaten down, and are fled apace**, and look not back: for fear was round about, saith the LORD."*

    B. Jeremiah 49:29 - *"Their (Chaldeans) tents and their flocks shall they take away: they shall take to themselves their curtains, and all their vessels, and their camels; and they shall cry unto them, **Fear is on every side**."*

V. **Fear not, and obey God no matter what.**

There are times when we are afraid to do the will of God because it just seems completely opposite of what we know to do, just doesn't make any sense, or we just don't understand it. Nevertheless, we need to obey

God's word no matter what. He knows best. Like Isaiah 55:9 says, His ways higher than your ways, and his thoughts than your thoughts.

   A.   Examples of those who obeyed God and believed in Him:

   1.   **Abraham** - Genesis 22:1-3 - *"¹And it came to pass after these things, that God did tempt Abraham, and said unto him, Abraham: and he said, Behold, here I am. ²And **he said, Take now thy son, thine only son Isaac, whom thou lovest, and get thee into the land of Moriah; and offer him there for a burnt offering** upon one of the mountains which I will tell thee of. ³And Abraham rose up early in the morning, and saddled his ass, and took two of his young men with him, and Isaac his son, and clave the wood for the burnt offering, and rose up, and went unto the place of which God had told him."* –

Abraham was ready to sacrifice his son even though it didn't make much sense in the natural. But he trusted God and he knew the one in whom he believed. It can be really scary to step out of our comfort zone, to step out in faith, but by doing that, we can prove our faithfulness to God. Abraham didn't ask a question, he just got up and go the next day. I pray such a faith, obedience and trust in God.

   2.   **Joseph** - Matthew 1:20 - *"But while he thought on these things, behold, the angel of the Lord appeared unto him in a dream, saying, Joseph, thou son of David, **fear not to take unto thee Mary thy wife**: for that which is conceived in her is of the Holy Ghost."*
   3.   **Moses' Parents** - Hebrews 11:23 - *"By faith Moses, when he was born, **was hid three months of his parents**, because they saw he was a proper child; and **they were not afraid** of the king's commandment."*
   4.   **Ananias** - Acts 9:10-17 - *"¹⁰And there was a certain disciple at Damascus, named **Ananias; and to him said the Lord** in a vision, Ananias. And he said, Behold, I am here, Lord. ¹¹And the Lord said unto him, **Arise,** and go into the street which is called Straight, **and enquire in the house of Judas for one called Saul, of Tarsus**: for, behold, he prayeth, ¹²And hath seen in a vision a man named Ananias coming in, and putting his hand on him, that he might receive his sight. ¹³Then Ananias answered, **Lord, I have heard by many of this man, how much evil he hath done to thy saints at Jerusalem:** ¹⁴And*

> here he hath authority from the chief priests to bind all that call on thy name. *15But the Lord said unto him, Go thy way: for he is a chosen vessel unto me*, to bear my name before the Gentiles, and kings, and the children of Israel: *16For I will shew him how great things he must suffer for my name's sake. 17And **Ananias went his way, and entered into the house**; and putting his hands on him said, Brother Saul, the Lord, even Jesus, that appeared unto thee in the way as thou camest, hath sent me, that thou mightest receive thy sight, and be filled with the Holy Ghost."*

In the past, Paul was killing Christians or anybody and everybody who spoke in the name of Jesus. It didn't make any sense to Ananias to go to Paul and talk to him about Jesus. It was pretty scary just to even think about doing it. But God knows the end from the beginning; He is the Alpha and the Omega, the Beginning and the End. We just need to trust in Him and do what He says, no matter what we see with our natural eyes, or what our own reasoning may be saying to us and then we won't be afraid.

    B.   Example of that which did not first obey and believe in God:

        1.   **Peter** - Acts 10:11-17 - *"11And saw heaven opened, and a certain vessel descending unto him, as it had been a great sheet knit at the four corners, and let down to the earth: 12Wherein were all manner of fourfooted beasts of the earth, and wild beasts, and creeping things, and fowls of the air. 13**And there came a voice to him, Rise, Peter; kill, and eat.** 14**But Peter said, Not so, Lord; for I have never eaten any thing that is common or unclean.** 15And the voice spake unto him again the second time, What God hath cleansed, that call not thou common. 16This was done thrice: and the vessel was received up again into heaven. 17Now while **Peter doubted in himself** what this vision which he had seen should mean, behold, the men which were sent from Cornelius had made enquiry for Simon's house, and stood before the gate."*

When we don't obey God, we will doubt in ourselves like Peter did. Still later Peter went to Cornelius' house. (Acts 10:28 *"And he said unto them, Ye know how that **it is an unlawful thing for a man that is a Jew to keep company**, or come unto one of another nation; **but God hath shewed me that I should not call any man common or unclean.**"*) Peter wasn't ready immediately to do God's will, he doubted himself at first, but in the end, he followed God's commandment. It's never too late to repent and do the will of God.

Over and over again Jesus did things that, at first didn't seem like it lined up with the laws of the Pharisees, like eating on the Sabbath day or talking to a Samaritan woman, etc. We should not be afraid to do anything that God asks us to do, even if we don't understand it. His ways are not our ways. Jesus said only believe.

Conclusion

In this chapter let me summarize all that God showed me concerning fear.

Fear of things or men is simply a lie. The devil and our own mind is the inventor of these lies. We should only fear God. First, the Word of God is light and truth and it exposes the lie of the devil and any other false voice. The enemy can even use the Word of God to make us afraid. He uses the Word to deceive us, just like he used the Word of God in the wilderness with Jesus, and in the garden with Adam and Eve. But if we really know God and His purpose in our lives, then we can easily reveal the lies of the devil.

Hebrews 13:5-6 says, *"Let your conversation be without covetousness; and **be content** with such things as ye have: for he hath said, I will never leave thee, nor forsake thee. **So that** <u>we may boldly say, The Lord is my helper</u>, **and I will not fear** what man shall do unto me."* We will go through the dealings of God until we reach the point that we will no longer walk in fear and can boldly say: *"The Lord is my helper, and I will not fear what man shall do unto me."* We see an example when the Israelites were afraid of Pharaoh's army at the Red sea. But after seeing God coming through for them, they believed and feared God respectfully, rather than men. *"And **Israel saw that great work which the LORD did** upon the Egyptians: and the people feared the LORD, and **believed the LORD**, and his servant Moses."* (Exodus 14:31)

Job is also a great example of this. The things he feared the most came upon him. And once that happened there was nothing left to fear anymore. God liberated him. Then God restored him and he received a double portion. This will happen to us also if we walk with God. The key is to walk with God. **Once Job faced his fears, there was nothing left to bind him.** God wants us to be without fear. **Living without fear is liberating**.

Jesus puts us through afflictions in this world so that, in the end, we can see that He is faithful no matter what. It's by this that He delivers us from fear; the fear of this world, fear of finances, losing somebody, losing control and so on. *"There is no fear in love; but perfect love casteth out fear: because fear hath torment. He that feareth is not made perfect in love."* (1 John 4:18) We can walk in the prefect love of God if we are without fear.

Fear has to be exposed. God uses affliction to expose it. After it is exposed, we can see that we don't have any reason to fear because it is just a lie from the devil or the product of our imagination. God's desire is that we would never fear anything, only Him. But even then, we fear Him in a respecting way. He only wants the devil to be afraid of Him. God is greater than anything and anyone and He is faithful and able to keep us.

Fear is bondage as we can read in Romans 8:15: *"For ye have not received the spirit of bondage again to fear;"* Then Hebrews 2:15 says, *"deliver them who through fear of death were all their lifetime subject to bondage."* Without fear, we reach a place of liberty. **The fear of this world, of our lives is the enemy of the faith of God.** Fear shows our lack of confidence and trust in God.

Can bad things happen to us? Sure it can, and it will, it might not seem joyous at the moment. But if you don't break the hedge around yourself it will yield the "peaceable fruit of righteousness." *"Now no chastening for the present seemeth to be joyous, but grievous: nevertheless afterward it yieldeth the peaceable fruit of righteousness unto them which are exercised thereby."* (Hebrews 12:11) Because ALL things work together for good to those who love God (Romans 8:28) and better is the end of a thing than the beginning thereof (Ecclesiastes 7:8). If we let God lead us, we won't fear of anything. Psalms 78:53 – *"And he **led them on safely, so that they feared not**: but the sea overwhelmed their enemies."*

It is not easy to get delivered from fear and most of the time it doesn't happen instantaneously. But don't get discouraged and faint not in your heart, but memorize God's words, and use them over and over again, and the time will come when you won't fear anymore. Fear is all around us, constantly trying to stop us from doing the will of God. Fear can paralyze us. As matter of fact, one of the meanings of fear means: falling as dead (Matthew 28:4). It paralyzes us. But be of good cheer; He that overcometh the world is with and within us! Don't give up fighting the good fight of faith. Just run to the stronghold when you are weak. God will take care of you and He will protect you. Never let the enemy and fear lead you astray from the road God put you on. Fear can be all around you, but if you trust in God, you can be sure that nothing will happen to you that isn't to further your walk in Jesus. Don't listen to those voices, words of the enemy, but only hear God's voice. Pay no attention to other words, don't even entertain them for a second, but cast them down immediately. Don't give into reasoning words, only listen to God. Those lying words just want to stop your purpose in God. Don't let them!

Let me finish with this; God said *"Fear ye not, neither be afraid: have not I told thee from that time, and have declared it? ye are even my witnesses. Is there a God beside me? yea, there is no God; I know not any."* (Isaiah 44:8) and Jesus said before He died, **"Peace I leave with you, my peace I give unto you: not as the world giveth, give I unto you. Let not your heart be troubled, neither let it be afraid."** (John 14:27)

Made in the USA
Middletown, DE
16 October 2021